ADVENTU

The
Airfield Game

based on Enid Blyton's
Five Go to Billycock Hill

Illustrated by Gary Rees

HODDER AND STOUGHTON
LONDON SYDNEY AUCKLAND TORONTO

British Library Cataloguing in Publication Data

The secret airfield game: adventure games book:.
    based on Enid Blyton's Five go to Billycock Hill.
    — (Famous Five adventure games)
    1. Adventure games— Juvenile literature
    I. Blyton, Enid, Five go to Billycock Hill
    II. Rees, Gary   III. Series
    793'.9   GV1203

    ISBN 0-340-39654-7

First published 1986
Second impression 1988

Published by Hodder and Stoughton Children's Books,
a division of Hodder and Stoughton Ltd,
Mill Road, Dunton Green, Sevenoaks, Kent TN13 2YJ

Photoset by Rowland Photosetting Ltd,
Bury St Edmunds, Suffolk

Printed in Great Britain by Hazell, Watson & Viney Ltd,
Member of BPCC plc,
Aylesbury, Bucks

You have often read about The Famous Five's adventures . . . now here's your chance to take part in one!

This time YOU are in charge. YOU have to work out the clues, read the maps, crack the codes. Whether The Five solve the mystery or not is in your hands.

You will not necessarily solve the mystery on your first attempt. It may well take several goes. Keep trying, though, and you will eventually be successful.

Even when you *have* solved the mystery, the game can still be played again. For there are many different routes to the solution – and each route involves different clues and adventures.

So, the game can be played over and over. As many times as you like!

HOW TO PLAY

To solve the mystery, you have to go with The Five on an adventure through the book. You do this by starting at PARAGRAPH ONE and then following the instructions to other paragraphs.

Many of the paragraphs will ask you to work out some sort of clue. You do not have to work out every one of the clues to solve the final mystery . . . but the more you manage, the more you're likely to be successful. The fewer clues you crack, the less chance of completing the adventure.

To help you work out the clues, there are several pieces of equipment available – a pair of binoculars, a compass, a map and a codebook. You can start with only *one* of these EQUIPMENT CARDS but you will often pick up others as the game goes along. Occasionally, however, you will be asked to give some up as well.

To hold your EQUIPMENT CARDS during the adventure, there is a RUCKSACK CARD. This will tell you exactly which EQUIPMENT CARDS you have for use at any one time (so, after they've helped in solving a particular clue, always remember to return them to your rucksack!). Any EQUIPMENT CARDS not in your rucksack **cannot be used or consulted** – and therefore should be kept out of play.

Of course, no Famous Five adventure could take place without provisions. You are therefore given three PICNIC CARDS. These are to be kept in the slit of the LUNCHBOX CARD.

Every time The Five eat or lose some of their provisions during the adventure, you must remove one of your PICNIC CARDS from the LUNCHBOX CARD. When there are no PICNIC CARDS left in your LUNCHBOX, the provisions have run out and so you cannot possibly continue with the adventure. The game is over and you will have to start again from the beginning.

READY TO START

The Famous Five are JULIAN (the biggest and eldest), DICK, GEORGE (real name Georgina, but she always wanted to be a boy), ANNE and George's dog, TIMMY.

A school friend of Julian's, Toby, has invited them to his farm for part of their summer holidays. The farm is in the heart of the wild Cornish countryside and so they are all very excited about it. On their arrival there, Toby proudly introduces them to his cousin, Jeff, who is a handsome young pilot. Jeff tells them that he is stationed at a military airfield a few miles from the farm but that they must keep this to themselves. This is because the airfield is a secret one, where lots of special planes are kept.

The Five really take to Jeff and so they are completely stunned when, a couple of days later, a news report comes on their radio. It is announced that Jeff has stolen a top secret jet from the airfield, and has flown it abroad to sell to the country's enemies! Toby likewise hears the report about Jeff being a traitor and rushes in on The Five, absolutely distraught. In floods of tears, he insists that his cousin would never dream of such a thing and that there had to be some other explanation for his sudden disappearance.

The Five can't think what other explanation there *could* be but they feel so sorry for Toby that they promise to do some investigating. The obvious place to start is at the airfield. So, they prepare to make an immediate visit to this secret military site . . .

To join them on this trip, you will first of all need to put on your rucksack. So pick out the RUCKSACK CARD and keep it near to you. You must now choose a piece of equipment to take with you. The Five each have a pair of binoculars, a compass, a map and a codebook – but you can start with only *one* of these. Which do you think would be the most useful? Insert the EQUIPMENT CARD you have chosen into the slit of your RUCKSACK CARD and keep the remaining three EQUIPMENT CARDS out of play until told you can pick them up.

Now for the provisions. Toby's mother kindly prepares for The Five a delicious picnic of sandwiches, cherry cake and ginger beer. Put the three PICNIC CARDS into the slit of the LUNCHBOX CARD. Don't forget to remove a picnic card every time The Five eat or lose some of their provisions.

Remember: when there are no PICNIC CARDS left in your LUNCHBOX, the adventure has to stop and you must start all over again.

Good Luck!

As the Five left Toby's farmhouse, they again promised him that they would do all they could to prove that his cousin was innocent. 'We don't believe he's a traitor either!' Julian told him with a kind pat on his shoulder. 'He seemed *far* too nice!' They waved Toby one last cheerful goodbye as they shut the farm gate behind them and set off for the airfield. After having walked a good half mile or so, however, they suddenly realised that they didn't know where the airfield was! 'Toby's bound to know,' said Dick. 'One of us will have to run back and ask him which direction to go!'

Throw the special FAMOUS FIVE DICE to decide who it's to be – then turn to the appropriate number. If you throw 'Mystery', you must turn to that number instead.

JULIAN thrown	go to 156
DICK thrown	go to 244
GEORGE thrown	go to 19
ANNE thrown	go to 120
TIMMY thrown	go to 190
MYSTERY thrown	go to 221

2

Having found due east on their compasses, The Five now set off in that direction. Anne turned round to give the gypsy woman a wave as they went. The woman might have *looked* a bit scary with her old shawl and missing teeth, but she had actually been rather nice! **Go to 104.**

3

The others took no notice of George's suggestion of taking a compass reading, though. 'The *next* time there's a mist, we'll jolly well stop right where we are until it clears!' Dick told her. Before they set off in the direction in which they had seen the jet, Julian proposed that they all have a drink of their ginger beer. There was still quite a walk ahead of them and so they could probably do with the refreshment!

Take a PICNIC CARD from your LUNCHBOX. Now go to 83.

4

Suddenly, as Dick was about to start decoding the message on the wall, a couple of airmen appeared in the hangar! He quickly hid behind some oil drums, waiting for them to leave. It looked as if they were going to stand there chatting all day, however, and so – with his heart in his mouth – he made a dash for it while they were facing the other way. **Go to 290.**

'No, it's this way, Timmy!' George called to him just as they were about to start walking along the railway line. 'You're going in the wrong direction!' Timmy continued to wander the *opposite* way along the line, though, seeming to follow some sort of scent. Suddenly he stopped, looking at one of the sleepers. 'What have you found, Timmy?' George asked excitedly as she ran up to him. When she reached the sleeper, she saw that someone had chalked a message on it! The message was in code, though, and so they were going to have to consult their codebooks.

Use your CODEBOOK CARD to find out what the message said by decoding the instruction below. If you don't have a CODEBOOK in your RUCKSACK, go to 93 instead.

As hard as The Five tried to persuade him, the sentry still refused to let them enter the airfield. They at last gave up and wandered off – but they continued to follow the barbed-wire fence round. They had reached the north side of the airfield when they suddenly spotted a small hole at the base of the fence! 'We could get into the airfield through *here*!' Julian suggested daringly. 'I know it's a very serious thing to do – and we'd be in awful trouble if we were caught – but what we're investigating is very serious too!' The others agreed it was worth the risk but George said there would be much less chance of being spotted if only *one* of them went. All they had to do now was wait for a volunteer!

Throw THE FAMOUS FIVE DICE to decide who it's to be.

JULIAN thrown	go to 22
DICK thrown	go to 133
GEORGE thrown	go to 276
ANNE thrown	go to 179
TIMMY thrown	go to 41
MYSTERY thrown	go to 72

Dick was just pointing his compass towards the airfield, ready to read its direction, when George said it wasn't necessary. 'If we could see the castle all the way from the airfield,' she told him rather pompously, 'we should be able to see the airfield all the way from the castle! So we don't need your compass reading, silly!' While Dick was irritably putting his compass away again, George took out her ginger beer. She was so pleased at having humbled Dick that she thought she would treat herself to a drink!

Take a PICNIC CARD from your LUNCHBOX. Now go to 107. (Remember: when there are no picnic cards left in your lunchbox the game is over, and you must start again.)

8

'Of course!' Dick suddenly exclaimed after a while. 'The obvious thing to do is to look up the caves on our maps. They're bound to be shown if they're a decent size!' So they all quickly slipped off their rucksacks, racing each other to be the first to spot the caves on their maps!

Use your MAP to find which square the caves are in (there's a 'Danger' sign there!) – then follow the instruction. If you don't have a MAP in your RUCKSACK, you'll have to guess which instruction to follow.

If you think A3	go to 96
If you think B4	go to 74
If you think A4	go to 150

9

'Those men have obviously dynamited the tunnel!' Julian cried with alarm. 'They must have spotted us entering the cave and decided to make sure we never got out again!' They all started to panic, wondering what they were going to do, but then Jeff told them that there was another tunnel leading from the cavern. 'See it? It's over there!' he remarked, pointing into the shadows. 'It's so narrow that I don't think the men noticed it. I only realised it was there myself because of the draught of air!' Although they couldn't be sure that the tunnel led anywhere, The Five immediately cheered up again, hurrying over to it.

Throw THE FAMOUS FIVE DICE to decide who is to lead down the tunnel.

JULIAN thrown	go to 261
DICK thrown	go to 199
GEORGE thrown	go to 65
ANNE thrown	go to 218
TIMMY thrown	go to 286
MYSTERY thrown	go to 49

10

'Oh, drat!' exclaimed Julian as he opened his compass. 'I'd forgotten that its face wouldn't show up in the dark!' Since none of them had a luminous compass, they decided they would just have to kick around for the lamp. As they were doing this, George suddenly tripped and dropped her lunchbox. The *good* news was that she had tripped over the lamp. Switching the lamp on, however, she saw the bad news. Her lunchbox had come open as it fell and most of her sandwiches were now covered in dirt!

Take a PICNIC CARD from your LUNCHBOX. Now go to 184.

11

The cave seemed to burrow further and further into the hill, narrowing down to a sort of tunnel. After a while, though, the tunnel suddenly divided. One branch went off to the left and the other to the right. They were just wondering which to take when Anne spotted a message chalked on the rocky ground. It read: *FOLLOW PATH WHICH LEADS SOUTH-EAST.* They immediately started searching for their compasses!

Use your COMPASS CARD to find south-east by placing exactly over the shape below – and with pointer touching north. Then go to the number that appears in the window. If you don't have a COMPASS in your RUCKSACK, you'll have to guess which of the numbers to go to.

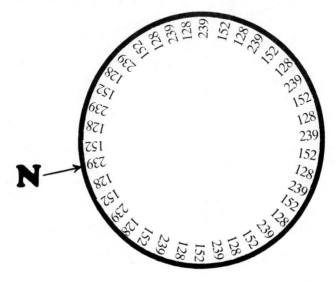

12

It was by now almost completely dark but they had still to reach the airfield. 'It can't be much further,' Jeff told them encouragingly, although he was secretly becoming rather anxious himself! Suddenly, they all heard a plane flying overhead. Jeff assumed it to be from his airfield but, glancing up, he saw that it was a type he didn't recognise. Furthermore, there was some sort of code painted on the underside of its wings! He quickly told the children to hand him one of their codebooks!

Use your CODEBOOK CARD to find out what the code on the plane's wings said by decoding the instruction below. If you don't have a CODEBOOK in your RUCKSACK, go to 33 instead.

13

'Look – there's a bird flying towards us!' George suddenly cried while Dick was still trying to find his binoculars. 'That proves the light *must* be coming from the outside!' So Dick quickly strapped his rucksack up again, slinging it on to his back and immediately leading the way forward. Anne was so delighted to see the bird that she took out a piece of her cake for it, crumbling it on to the ground!

Take a PICNIC CARD from your LUNCHBOX. Now go to 32.

'You see that large stone cross on the hill over there!' George suddenly exclaimed with inspiration, pointing to her right. 'Why don't we look it up on our maps as a guide to where we are? That will at least be a *start* in trying to find the airfield!' The others agreed it was a good idea and so they all hurriedly slipped off their rucksacks to look for their maps.

Use your MAP to find which square the stone cross is in – then follow the instruction. If you don't have a MAP in your RUCKSACK, you'll have to guess which instruction to follow.

If you think E3   go to 300
If you think D4   go to 66
If you think E4   go to 16

15

Before they had a chance to take out their maps, however, they suddenly heard a faint whining sound in the distance. The children all wondered what it was and Jeff said that it came from the airfield. 'It's an alarm for when the airfield is under attack,' he said. 'They always test it round about this time of the day.' The sound had come from behind the hills over to their right and so they immediately set off in that direction! *Go to 35.*

16

'Wait a minute!' Jeff suddenly exclaimed as the children were still searching their maps for the stone cross. 'I've just noticed that radio mast over there in the distance. See its red light flashing? Well, I'm sure that's the one just behind the airfield!' So he suggested they immediately head towards *that*, forgetting about looking at their maps. 'Anyone like a sandwich?' Anne asked on the way. 'It will make my lunchbox a little lighter.' She found the others only too pleased to help out!

Take a PICNIC CARD from your LUNCHBOX. Now go to 12.

George insisted on sitting in the front of the jeep, with the others all piling into the back. Moments later, the commander was driving the jeep through the airfield's gates and across the rough countryside. Suddenly, though, he slammed on the brakes! 'Blow! I think I must have made a wrong turn somewhere!' he exclaimed. 'I'm sure that reservoir over there isn't on the way to the ruined castle!' He asked the children to look it up on their maps to find out where they were.

Use your MAP to find which square the reservoir is in – then follow the instruction. If you don't have a MAP in your RUCKSACK, you'll have to guess which instruction to follow.

If you think D3	go to 189
If you think E4	go to 110
If you think D4	go to 86

Just as the two men were about to have their masks ripped off them, however, they both broke free and ran for their jeep. Timmy helped Jeff and the commander chase after them but the men just managed to start the engine in time. 'Blow! We've lost them!' the commander exclaimed with annoyance as the men quickly disappeared into the night before he could start their own jeep. 'Still, we've got our jet back – that's the main thing,' he added. 'And I dare say those men will try and steal it again one day. When they do, we'll be there waiting for them!' *So will we*, thought The Five, all together!

Your adventure wasn't quite successful. If you would like another attempt at solving the mystery, you must start the game again at paragraph one. Try choosing a different EQUIPMENT CARD this time to see if it gives you any more luck.

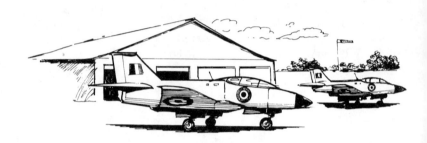

19

'It's best if I go back,' George offered, 'because I'm the fastest runner!' Julian and Dick were about to contradict this – they were both a lot faster than George, but they decided to keep quiet about it. If George wanted to go all the way back to the farmhouse, then let her! It was a good half hour before George returned, looking absolutely exhausted! 'Toby says we should keep following this track until it divides,' she panted, 'then take the left branch.' Julian suggested they look up where the track divided on their maps so they would know how much further it was.

Do you have a MAP in your RUCKSACK? If so, use it to find out in which square the track from the farmhouse divides – then follow the instruction. (Remember to put the MAP back in your

RUCKSACK afterwards.) If you don't have one, you'll have to guess which instruction to follow.

If you think A2	go to 55
If you think A1	go to 174
If you think B2	go to 87

20

'Research?' the other man asked with a nasty chuckle. 'No, we breed them for money. Some of these butterflies are worth a fortune when we've stuck a pin through them!' The Five all thought it very cruel of the men just to do it for the money, and decided to leave the butterfly farm. It looked as if they were just about to be evicted from it anyway! They didn't have to walk much further when they spotted several brightly-coloured caravans ahead. 'It looks like a gypsy camp!' remarked Dick. 'Let's go and ask there which direction the airfield is. Come on – we'll make it into a race!'

Throw THE FAMOUS FIVE DICE to decide who is to reach the gypsy camp first.

JULIAN thrown	go to 38
DICK thrown	go to 267
GEORGE thrown	go to 89
ANNE thrown	go to 213
TIMMY thrown	go to 145
MYSTERY thrown	go to 176

It had grown so windy that Anne had a problem keeping her map open while she looked up the stone archway. She therefore had the good idea of anchoring it down with her ginger beer bottle. Or was it such a good idea – because she forgot to shut her lunchbox lid after she took the bottle out! As she was studying the map, she suddenly noticed several large crows out of the corner of her eye. They were busy pecking away at her sandwiches!

Take a PICNIC CARD from your LUNCHBOX. Now go to 83.

22

As the eldest, Julian thought *he* had better volunteer to go through the hole. The others watched him squeeze between the sharp ends of wire and then dart across the concrete towards one of the hangars. 'Oh, Julian, be careful!' Anne anxiously whispered to herself as they saw him creep inside the hangar. While they waited tensely for him to return, Dick suggested looking up the airfield on their maps. It would be a way of occupying themselves!

Use your MAP to find out which square the airfield is in – then follow the instruction. If you don't have a MAP in your RUCKSACK, you'll have to guess which instruction to follow.

If you think E3	go to 82
If you think D3	go to 147
If you think D4	go to 279

23

'Stop brushing my legs, Timmy!' Julian told him irritably as they now left the hill with the beacon behind. 'Can't you walk a little further away?' Timmy continued to walk right on Julian's heels, though, and Julian crossly turned round to have another word with him. It was then that he saw *why* Timmy was there. His tongue was delightedly catching some drips that were leaking from the bottom of his lunchbox! 'Oh no, it must be my ginger beer that's leaking,' Julian exclaimed as he opened his lunchbox up to investigate. 'I couldn't have screwed the bottle-cap on properly!'

Take a PICNIC CARD from your LUNCHBOX. Now go to 236.

24

It was so dark inside the wood that they all became a little nervous. 'I wish we'd hurry up and reach the other side,' said Anne. 'It's almost like night-time!' She suddenly grabbed Julian's arm as she heard a crackling in the undergrowth a short way to their right. 'There's someone there!' she wailed, covering her eyes with her other hand. However, she soon felt Julian gently remove her hand from her eyes, chuckling as he did so. 'Why, it's just a deer!' she giggled as she saw what it was. She was so relieved that she took out one of her salad sandwiches, leaving it on the ground for the beautiful animal.

Take a PICNIC CARD from your LUNCHBOX. Now go to 163.

25

'Here it is!' George suddenly exclaimed as they were all studying their maps to find the end of the railway line. 'Near the top right corner – can you see?' The others soon located it too and so, now they had found out where they were, they continued on their way. For a long while the ruined castle seemed to get no closer but then it gradually grew clearer. In another half hour they should have reached it! *Go to 107.*

26

As the children were thinking, Anne suddenly noticed a rough arrow gouged into the ground. It looked as if it had been scraped by the heel of someone's shoe! 'Hey, maybe this arrow was made by Jeff when his two abductors weren't looking!' she exclaimed as she pointed it out to the others. 'If it was, then it's probably to show which direction the caves are!' The others agreed this could well be likely and so they decided to find out the direction the arrow pointed on their compasses. All they had to do then was follow their compasses!

Use your COMPASS CARD to find the arrow's direction by placing exactly over the shape below – and with pointer touching north. Then go to the number that appears in the window. If you don't have a COMPASS in your RUCKSACK, you'll have to guess which of the numbers to go to.

As they were slipping off their rucksacks to get their binoculars, however, Dick noticed some 'white' hills in the distance! 'Oh, so that's what Jeff meant by white hills!' he remarked. 'They're heaps of white waste from china clay pits. There are meant to be quite a lot of them in this part of the country.' Before setting off towards the strange-coloured hills, they decided to have a quick sandwich each. It looked quite a walk ahead of them!

Take a PICNIC CARD from your LUNCHBOX. Now go to 96.

28

Quickly consulting their codebooks, they worked out the message on the lamp as: *THIS IS THE PROPERTY OF PATRICK GRINGLE*. 'You know what that means, don't you?' Dick asked excitedly. 'It means that Patrick Gringle must be the name of one of Jeff's abductors! It's my guess that, after leaving Jeff somewhere in the cave, they dropped this lamp on their way out again!' Anne had only led them a short way further when her lamp shone on a small compass. 'I bet this belongs to one of those men as well!' she said as she bent down to pick it up.

If you don't already have it, put the COMPASS CARD into your RUCKSACK. Now go to 184.

29

As Dick was taking his map out, however, he accidentally knocked George's lunchbox. She had put it beside her on the wall . . . but now, thanks to Dick's carelessness, it was suddenly floating in the canal below! 'Quick, help me try and rescue it,' she cried as she ran down the bridge to the bank. She lay flat on her tummy, stretching out her arm towards the lunchbox. Just as it looked as if she was about to reach it, though, the lunchbox began to sink, weighed down by all the water that had got inside it. 'There goes all my picnic!' she wailed as it disappeared in a stream of bubbles.

Take a PICNIC CARD from your LUNCHBOX. Now go to 168.

'East is over *that* way,' said George, pointing to her right, when she was the first to find it on her compass. As they now hurried in that direction, Dick told Jeff that he had better ask his jets to make less noise in future. 'Otherwise, we'll all be drinking a glass of butter at breakfast!' he chuckled. ***Go to 254.***

Jeff said they didn't really have time to look up their maps, because it was essential they reached the airfield as quickly as possible. 'In fact, I think we'd better try running for a bit,' he added anxiously. 'I know you must all be tired but this is really very very important!' There was by now so little light, however, that running didn't prove at all easy and they hadn't gone far when Dick tripped, dropping his lunchbox. 'Blow! I think my ginger beer bottle's broken!' he moaned as he noticed liquid dripping out at the corner.

Take a PICNIC CARD from your LUNCHBOX. Now go to 67.

Much to everyone's relief and joy, the tunnel at last emerged into daylight. It wasn't the bright daylight they were expecting, though, because they had been so long in the caves that it was now nearly evening! 'We'd better get a move on,' Jeff said briskly as they squeezed through a large gap in the rock to the outside, 'or we're never going to get back to the airfield in time! The problem is – which way is it? Anyone got any ideas?'

Throw THE FAMOUS FIVE DICE to decide who is to come up with a suggestion.

JULIAN thrown	go to 109
DICK thrown	go to 273
GEORGE thrown	go to 14
ANNE thrown	go to 77
TIMMY thrown	go to 210
MYSTERY thrown	go to 129

By the time the children were ready with their codebooks, though, the plane had disappeared into the night. As they disappointedly put their codebooks away again, Julian asked Jeff what he thought the plane was doing there. 'I'm not sure,' Jeff replied uneasily, 'but I can't help feeling it was up to no good!' The Five had rather come to this conclusion as well, and their throats were so dry with the anxiety that Dick gave them all a drink of his ginger beer before they continued on their way.

Take a PICNIC CARD from your LUNCHBOX. Now go to 67. (Remember: when there are no picnic cards left in your lunchbox the game is over, and you must start again.)

34

Reading their compasses, the children told the commander that it was roughly in the direction of the moon. 'We're lucky the moon's so bright,' the commander remarked as he sped across the rough countryside towards it. 'It means that we can drive without putting our headlights on. We don't want those men to spot us before we can get close enough!' *Go to 111.*

35

It had been a good hour since they had left the tunnel and they still hadn't reached the airfield. 'We've got to get there soon,' Dick remarked anxiously, glancing up at the sky. 'Look, it's going to be pitch black before long!' They had only gone a little further, however, when they spotted some tiny lights ahead. 'I wonder if they're the airfield's runway lights,' Jeff said hopefully. 'Someone pass me a pair of binoculars, will they, so I can check?'

Use your BINOCULARS CARD to try and see if it is the airfield by placing exactly over the shape below – then follow the instruction. If you don't have BINOCULARS in your RUCK-SACK, go to 172 instead.

36

Just as Julian was about to look for the stones on his map, however, he suddenly found he couldn't see! 'I'm sorry about that,' the commander told him, 'but I've just dimmed the jeep's headlights. We should be approaching the ruined castle soon and I want to make sure those men don't spot us!' ***Go to 86.***

By the time the children had produced a pair of binoculars, however, the other jeep was close enough for them to see. There were two masked men inside and someone in a flying jacket! 'That's them!' Jeff whispered tensely. 'The two men who abducted me! The other one's obviously the foreign pilot.' *Go to 264.*

Julian won the race to the gypsy camp, immediately asking one of the gypsies there if they were going in the right direction for the airfield. The gypsy told him that they were, saying that they should follow that track for another two miles or so. They had walked about a quarter of this distance when Anne happened to glance behind her. 'Hey, look – there's someone watching us from that hill back there,' she exclaimed nervously. They all shielded their eyes, trying to see who it was, but the person was too far away. 'I know, we'll use our binoculars!' George suggested.

Use your BINOCULARS CARD to try and identify the person on the hill by placing exactly over the shape below – then follow the instruction. If you don't have BINOCULARS in your RUCKSACK, go to 81 instead.

```
  G Q Q    O  S  R  U  S   P  N T  M L  O
H G      T L      W N O R N   SS T E  U
N  S R G  IN  A G A   A  Y      X U U  E
F N O M  L  N I H       E U C E  A  R        L
```

'Here's the butterfly farm,' said Anne proudly, as she was the first to find it on her map. 'Look, just above the tip of my finger!' They then found Toby's cottage on the map as well, working it out as about two miles away. 'Is that all?' moaned George. 'It's funny how it always seems you've walked much further than you actually have!' *Go to 257.*

40

Having taken out their codebooks, they now prepared to decode the message on the photograph but, before they did, Dick had a quick drink of his ginger beer. The excitement of it had made him thirsty! 'Right, let's begin,' he said eagerly, putting the ginger beer bottle on top of the photograph to stop it blowing away. Unfortunately, though, he hadn't screwed the cap on as tightly as he had thought – and, even more unfortunately, George accidentally knocked the bottle! Not only did Dick lose all his ginger beer but the surface coating of the photograph immediately began to dissolve, making the message unreadable. They now wouldn't be able to decode it after all!

Take a PICNIC CARD from your LUNCHBOX. Now go to 83.

'No, *you* can't go!' the children all laughed as Timmy made it perfectly clear that *he* wanted to be the one to crawl through the fence and explore the airfield. When they thought about it, though, they decided that perhaps it wasn't such a bad idea after all. 'If any of the airfield people spot him,' Julian argued, 'then we could just say that he ran off. It would cause a lot less trouble than if one of us was spotted!' So they finally agreed to let Timmy go, anxiously watching him dart across the concrete towards the nearest of the hangars. Not long afterwards he emerged again, checking the coast was clear before making a dash to the next building. He was soon so far away that the children could hardly see him, so Dick suggested taking out their binoculars to follow his movements.

Use your BINOCULARS CARD to watch Timmy by placing exactly over the shape below – then follow the instruction. If you don't have BINOCULARS in your RUCKSACK, go to 115 instead.

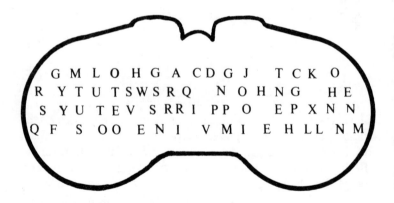

```
  G M L O H G A C D G J     T C K O
R Y T U T S W S R Q   N O H N G   H E
 S Y U T E V S R R I  PP O   E P X N N
Q F S O O E N I   V M I   E H L L N M
```

'Where are we going?' the others all asked bewilderedly as Julian now quickly led them away from the airfield fence. 'Why, the ruined castle, of course!' he replied. 'Don't you see? The jet that that message referred to is almost certainly Jeff's jet, the one he went missing in. If we can *find* the jet, we might be able to make more sense of all of this!' The ruined castle was just about visible in the far distance but it was going to be a long, long walk. They had only done a short part of this walk when they reached a disused railway line. Since the railway line ran in the right direction, they decided to walk along it.

Throw THE FAMOUS FIVE DICE to decide who is to lead the way along the railway line.

JULIAN thrown	go to 215
DICK thrown	go to 123
GEORGE thrown	go to 193
ANNE thrown	go to 270
TIMMY thrown	go to 60
MYSTERY thrown	go to 5

43

They hadn't walked far from the end of the railway line when they spotted an old copper mine to their left. 'Ah, that explains what the railway was for!' Dick remarked. 'It was obviously used to transport the copper. I *thought* the area seemed far too deserted for it to be a passenger line!' He started to watch where he trod, thinking he might come across a lump of copper in the grass. He didn't find any copper but he *did* find an old compass! Since it was in perfectly good condition, he decided to take it with him as a spare.

If you don't already have it, put the COMPASS CARD into your RUCKSACK. Now go to 236.

44

Having found the river on their maps, they now set off again. 'It was fun going on those stepping-stones, wasn't it?' George asked. 'I think it's a much better way of crossing a river than walking over a bridge!' Timmy, though, knew of an even better way and was disappointed that he hadn't been allowed to try it. His way was to splash right through the water! *Go to 181.*

45

The others thought getting out their binoculars would just waste time, though. They might as well wait until they actually *reached* the castle now. So Dick left his binoculars where they were, in his rucksack, joining the others in a run for the final stretch to the castle. George tried to run a bit *too* hard, however, because she suddenly tripped and went sprawling across the ground. Fortunately, she wasn't hurt, but an ominous rattling sound from her lunchbox told her that her ginger beer bottle had smashed!

Take a PICNIC CARD from your LUNCHBOX. Now go to 107. (Remember: when there are no picnic cards left in your lunchbox the game is over, and you must start again.)

While they were still trying to think how they could find their way to Billycock Caves, George suddenly noticed an arrow chalked on the stone archway they had just come through. Above the arrow were the letters B.C. 'I bet B.C. stands for Billycock Caves!' she cried after she had pointed it out to the others. 'The arrow must have been put there by Jeff to show in which direction they are!' The others agreed with her deduction and so they all quickly went to their rucksacks for their compasses so they could work out the arrow's direction. They would then still know which way to go even after they had left the castle!

Use your COMPASS CARD to find the chalked arrow's direction by placing exactly over the shape below – and with pointer touching north. Then go to number that appears in the window. If you don't have a COMPASS in your RUCKSACK, you'll have to guess which of the numbers to go to.

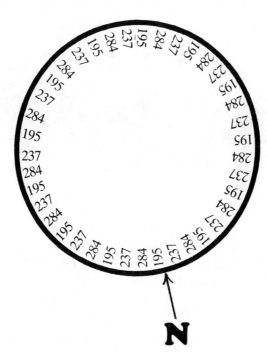

N

As Dick was eagerly searching for his binoculars, though, George told him that the cave would be too dark for them. 'Yes, I was forgetting about that!' he tutted. 'I suppose we'll just have to take pot-luck with the caves after all!' So he continued walking into that cave, which grew blacker and blacker as he did so. Julian was just about to say that they should have brought their torches with them when he tripped on a bicycle lamp. 'Hey, it works!' he exclaimed as he switched it on, shining it all round. It was a pity that he didn't shine it at his feet. If he had, he would have seen that his compass had slipped out of his rucksack!

*If you have it, remove the **COMPASS CARD** from your **RUCKSACK**. Now go to 11.*

Before Dick had time to look through the binoculars, though, there was an enormous explosion back down the tunnel. The shock made Anne knock hard against the tunnel wall, causing her ginger beer bottle to shatter! But it had a far more serious result. Part of the tunnel fell in with the explosion and their way out was now blocked by a massive pile of smoking rocks!

*Take a **PICNIC CARD** from your **LUNCHBOX**. Now go to 9.*

'Hey, take a look at this!' Julian exclaimed, just as they were about to enter the tunnel. 'It's a screwed-up letter. It says that the pilot will be dropped at the white cross!' Jeff immediately took the letter from him, examining it closely. 'It must have fallen from the pocket of one of those two men,' he told them thoughtfully. 'The pilot who's to fly the jet abroad is obviously going to arrive by parachute!' He then asked the children to look up the white cross on their maps so they would know where it was.

Use your MAP to find which square the white cross is in – then follow the instruction. If you don't have a MAP in your RUCKSACK, you'll have to guess which instruction to follow.

If you think B1	go to 252
If you think C1	go to 153
If you think D1	go to 97

'Oh no, the jet's gone!' George sighed when they were all ready with their compasses. 'We were so busy searching through our rucksacks that none of us remembered to keep an eye on it!' Jeff told them not to worry, though, *he* had kept an eye on it. 'It went behind that hill over there,' he said, pointing. 'So all you have to do is take a compass reading of that instead!' ***Go to 280.***

51

'No, you don't be wanting any of them fancy instr'ments!' the farmer chided them when they had produced their compasses. 'You tells east just by looking at the sky. You see that setting sun over there? Well, that's west – so east must be exactly opposite!' Before they all set off in this direction, Dick gave the farmer a couple of sandwiches for his help, and for the useful tip they had learnt from him!

Take a PICNIC CARD from your LUNCHBOX. Now go to 254.

52

Anne was being tossed up and down so much by the jeep, however, that she found it impossible to study her map! But it hardly mattered because they suddenly spotted the ruined castle ahead. Jeff told the commander to stop the jeep a couple of hundred metres short of it, well out of sight, while he crept up to the castle to check on the situation. 'The jet's still there, fortunately!' he told them when he at last returned. 'Which means that the foreign pilot can't have been brought here yet.' Hardly had he finished speaking, though, than a jeep appeared in the distance. They could just make out two masked men and a third man in a flying jacket. These men were obviously the ones they were after! *Go to 264.*

Dick climbed into the front of the jeep, sitting between the commander and Jeff. The commander told them all to sit tight as he now drove the jeep out of the airfield's gates and across the rough countryside. As they sped along, bumping up and down, Dick suddenly noticed something white in the sky. 'I think that might be a parachute!' he said excitedly, quickly feeling through his rucksack for his binoculars.

Use your BINOCULARS CARD to see whether it is a parachute or not by placing exactly over the shape below – then follow the instruction. If you don't have BINOCULARS in your RUCKSACK, go to 212 instead.

'It says that this is the property of Miguel Povlosky,' Dick said when he had quickly decoded the message on the parachute. He and the rest of The Five all wondered who Miguel Povlosky was but the commander said that he must be the foreign pilot who was coming to fly the jet abroad. 'This parachute proves that he's already here,' he added anxiously. 'He must have been dropped from the air and is presumably now being transported to the ruined castle. So we'd better get moving or we're going to be too late!' *Go to 111.*

55

The Five had walked quite a way further across the countryside when they arrived at a little cottage. At its side was a huge glasshouse full of plants and they assumed it must be some sort of nursery. 'Let's see if there's anyone about so we can check we're still going in the right direction,' Julian suggested. Walking round the glasshouse, they suddenly spotted an old man working away inside. They were just about to open the door to go and speak to him, when someone shouted at them from behind. 'Leave that door alone!' the angry voice ordered. *Go to 198.*

56

While they were unstrapping their rucksacks to look for their codebooks, however, there was a sudden shower of rain. They therefore quickly looked for their anoraks instead – which were, of course, right down at the bottom! 'Oh no, the rain's stopped now!' Dick moaned as soon as he had put his on. When they had packed their anoraks away again, they turned their attention back to the notebook. No one had thought to close it, however, and the rain had made the ink run. The code was now completely unreadable! *Go to 257.*

They had gone quite a way further on their journey towards the airfield when a jet came flying right above their heads! 'Hey, that's exactly the sort of jet that Toby said Jeff flew,' Dick exclaimed, when it seemed to hover for a while. 'You don't think it *is* Jeff, do you? Perhaps he lost his direction on some night exercise and has just found his way back again!' He quickly told them all to take out their binoculars so they could try and see into the jet's cockpit.

Use your BINOCULARS CARD to try and see if this is Jeff or not by placing exactly over the shape below – then follow the instruction. If you don't have BINOCULARS in your RUCK-SACK, go to 71 instead.

Studying their maps, the children eventually found the folly on them. 'Look, it's called Sir William's Arch,' George said. 'So it must have been a person called Sir William who built this useless thing.' As they put their maps away again, however, Julian pointed out that the monument wasn't that useless. 'After all, it helped us find out where we are, didn't it?' he chuckled. *Go to 83.*

'Here is a ruined castle, about five miles away!' Julian said, studying his map, after Anne had told them about the message. They then all gave Anne a pat on the back, telling her how courageous she had been. 'And observant!' they added.
Go to 224.

Timmy led the way along the disused railway line, bounding from sleeper to sleeper. 'Not too fast!' the others called after him. 'We can't keep up!' Timmy didn't seem to realise that they had rucksacks and lunchboxes to carry as well! After about half a mile, they suddenly reached the end of the railway line, arriving at some buffers and a few ramshackle huts. 'Let's see if it's shown on our maps,' Dick suggested. 'It will tell us where we are!'

Use your MAP to find which square the end of the railway line is in – then follow the instruction. If you don't have a MAP in your RUCKSACK, you'll have to guess which instruction to follow.

If you think E3	go to 236
If you think E2	go to 43
If you think D2	go to 258

Julian looked both puzzled and grave when he had decoded the message on the slip of paper. 'Well, come on,' Dick demanded impatiently, 'what does it say?' Julian put the slip of paper carefully into his pocket before answering. 'It says that the gun is to be used in stealing the jet,' he replied soberly. 'It doesn't say who left the gun-case here – or who it was for – but the fact that the gun is now missing from the case suggests that it probably *was* used for that!'
Go to 181.

'So it was *you* who wrote that message!' Julian exclaimed to Jeff. 'That's how we started to follow this trail. And, when we reached the ruined castle, we found your diary saying that you had been taken to these caves!' Jeff praised the cleverness of The Five, saying that he would probably have remained there for ever otherwise! 'But rescuing me is not what's important,' he added seriously. 'We've got to hurry back to the airfield and inform my commander of all this. Those two men are planning to take an enemy pilot to the ruined castle so he can fly the jet abroad. It's to happen on Friday night. Today must be Friday, isn't that right?' The children were just about to confirm this when Dick thought he heard voices from back down the tunnel. He immediately went for his binoculars to see if there was anyone there!

Use your BINOCULARS CARD to see if there is anyone there yourself by placing exactly over the shape below – then follow the instruction. If you don't have BINOCULARS in your RUCK-SACK, go to 48 instead.

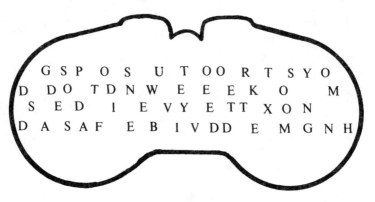

```
  G  SP   O   S    U   T  OO   R   T   S Y O
D   DO   TDN  W   E    E    E  K    O        M
 S    E  D    I    E  VY   E TT   X  O N
D   A   S A F    E   B   I V  DD    E   M  G  N H
```

They all held their binoculars to their eyes, slowly looking round with them. Suddenly, Dick stopped! 'I think I've spotted them!' he cried. 'See that small hill over there? There are two large holes at its base. I bet they're the caves!' When they had focused on the hill as well, the others agreed with Dick and they quickly returned to the bottom of the tower in order to set off in that direction! *Go to 96.*

64

'LOOK – DIRECTLY – BELOW – THIS – MESSAGE,' Dick said slowly as he gradually decoded the message on the wall. No sooner had he finished decoding it than the others did exactly that, holding the candle to the ground. 'There's a compass!' Julian exclaimed, as its glass face reflected the candle's flickering light. 'And look, there's Jeff's initials on the back – J.T.! He must have left his compass here in case anyone came searching for him. So they could later find their way out again, I expect!'

If you don't already have it, put the COMPASS CARD into your RUCKSACK. Now go to 11.

65

'Do you think it *will* eventually come out somewhere, Jeff?' George asked anxiously over her shoulder as she led them along the tunnel. They had been following it for a good half hour now but there was still no sign of the outside. 'Well, it can't go on forever,' Jeff replied comfortingly. 'I know! Why don't you take out your compass so you can see which direction it's leading. We can then perhaps work out roughly where we are!'

Use your COMPASS CARD to find the tunnel's direction by placing exactly over the shape below – and with pointer touching north. Then go to the number that appears in the window. If you don't have a COMPASS in your RUCKSACK, you'll have to guess which of the numbers to go to.

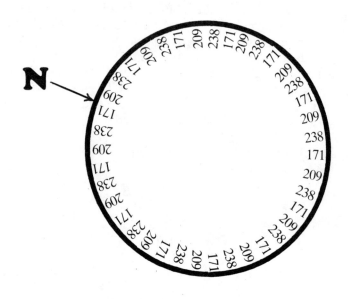

'So if the stone cross is here,' Jeff said thoughtfully, as Julian showed it to him on his map, 'then we must be round about here – near this patch of green. I think it's just a matter of walking east for a couple of miles – towards that radio mast in the distance.' They immediately set off towards the radio mast but they hadn't gone far when Julian stopped to pick something up from the grass. 'Yes, I thought it was!' he exclaimed. 'It's a compass! We'll take it with us as a spare!'

If you don't already have it, put the COMPASS CARD into your RUCKSACK. Now go to 12.

67

They at last reached the airfield, Jeff immediately leading them all to his commander's office. As they entered, the commander looked as if he had just seen a ghost! 'Jeff!' he exclaimed, scarcely able to believe his eyes. 'What on earth are you doing here? We all thought you had disappeared abroad with your jet!' Jeff proceeded to tell him what had *really* happened to him, though, and how The Famous Five had cleverly come to his rescue . . . *Go to 117.*

68

They were just about to study their maps for the stones when Anne came panting back again. 'Toby says we've gone in the wrong direction,' she said, puffing. 'Remember where this track forked a little way back? Well, we should have taken the left branch instead of the right one.' Before they returned to the other branch, Anne had a long drink of her ginger beer. All that running had made her hot!

Take a PICNIC CARD from your LUNCHBOX. Now go to 130.

Anne reached the farmer first, with the others just a short way behind. When they asked the farmer if they were going in the right direction for the airfield, he nodded his head. 'Before you be off, though,' he added, producing a little plastic container from his pocket, 'what do any of you makes of this thing 'ere? I found it in me fields!' ***Go to 200.***

70

Flicking through his codebook, Julian decoded the message on the binoculars as: *USE THESE TO OBSERVE THE JETS AT THE AIRFIELD*. He immediately reached into his pocket for fifty pence, paying the gypsy for them. As they continued on their way, George asked Julian why he had changed his mind about buying the binoculars. 'That message suggested they were used for spying,' he explained gravely. 'So I thought we'd better take them with us to hand in to the authorities. There might be fingerprints on them!'

If you don't already have it, put the BINOCULARS CARD into your RUCKSACK. Now go to 274.

71

By the time they were ready with their binoculars, however, the jet was gone! 'Well, I doubt whether it was Jeff anyway,' Julian said, being realistic. 'The jet wasn't flying *towards* the airfield but *away*

from it. I think we were just trying to give ourselves some hope!'
Before they started walking again, George suggested they have a
quick sandwich. It seemed as if they hadn't eaten for hours!

Take a PICNIC CARD from your LUNCHBOX. Now go to 83.

They were still waiting for someone to volunteer to slip through the
hole when they saw a scrap of paper come blowing towards them
across the airfield. It caught on the barbed wire right at the top of the
fence, showing that there was a message written on it! It was in
bright red ink, quite clear to read, but it was also in code. So they
quickly went to their rucksacks for their codebooks!

*Use your CODEBOOK CARD to find out what the message
said by decoding the instruction below. If you don't have a
CODEBOOK in your RUCKSACK, go to 293 instead.*

'It says that these wire-cutters are to be used to cut a hole in the fence,' Julian slowly decoded after Anne had passed him her codebook. They wondered which fence it was referring to but then Dick suddenly thought of the airfield fence! 'Hey, you don't think it was the hole we found, do you?' he asked excitedly. 'Perhaps someone had cut it deliberately and then dropped the wire-cutters here where no one would suspect them!' The others all quietly pondered this possibility as they continued on their way. *Go to 116.*

74

As soon as they had found the caves on their maps, they prepared to set off in that direction. Timmy seemed to want something to eat first, though, sniffing at George's lunchbox. To begin with, George refused him but then the children realised that he hadn't had anything for a while. And come to think of it, neither had they! So they decided to sit down for a quick picnic. 'And it really *must* be a quick one,' Dick insisted as he opened his lunchbox, 'because Jeff's life could be in great danger!'

Take a PICNIC CARD from your LUNCHBOX. Now go to 96.

75

Timmy bravely led the way into the cave, the others keeping close behind! It soon became so dark, however, that they began to worry about how they were going to see. 'Why didn't we think to bring our torches with us?' Dick sighed, wanting to kick himself. Just at that moment though, they noticed a message on the cave wall. It was written in a special sort of paint that glowed in the dark and read: *FOR LAMP, WALK 12 PACES SOUTH-EAST*. The children immediately slipped off their rucksacks so they could feel for their compasses!

*Use your **COMPASS CARD** to find south-east by placing exactly over the shape below – and with pointer touching north. Then go to the number that appears in the window. If you don't have a **COMPASS** in your **RUCKSACK**, you'll have to guess which of the numbers to go to.*

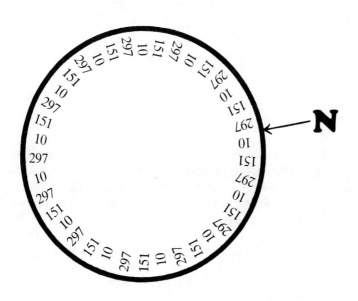

While the others were looking for their codebooks, though, Julian suddenly noticed a tiny gleam of light further up the tunnel. 'Hey, that must be the outside!' he exlaimed excitedly. 'Come on, let's just forget about the code and keep moving!' As they were hurrying along, Dick took a sandwich from his lunchbox, passing it forward to Jeff. 'Have one of my delicious ham and pickle sandwiches,' he told him. 'You can't have eaten for nearly two whole days!'

Take a PICNIC CARD from your LUNCHBOX. Now go to 32.

77

'Look, there's a canal over there!' Anne exclaimed suddenly, pointing a short way to her right. 'We could look it up on our maps to find out exactly where we are!' Jeff said it was a good idea – but they didn't know which *part* of the canal this was. He therefore suggested they follow the canal for a while until they reached something more specific, like a bridge or tunnel. 'This should do!' he remarked a short while later as they arrived at a lock. 'Right – maps everyone!'

Use your MAP to find which square the canal lock is in – then follow the instruction. If you don't have a MAP in your RUCKSACK, you'll have to guess which instruction to follow.

If you think B3	go to 201
If you think C3	go to 118
If you think B2	go to 154

Just as George was about to leave the hangar, though, she heard a couple of pilots approach! She quickly crouched down behind a work-bench in the corner. 'I wonder if I dropped my cigarettes in here,' one of them said as they entered. 'Yes, here they are – on the floor!' As he bent down to pick up the cigarettes, however, he suddenly noticed the chalked message George had found. 'What's all this about?' he asked. *'Five miles north-west of here* – that's the ruined castle, isn't it? Anyway, I don't suppose it means anything, so I might as well rub it off!' Much to George's relief, the two pilots now left the hangar and she made a dash back to the others at the fence. Thanks to that pilot, they didn't need to find north-west on their compasses now. What George definitely *did* need, though, was a long drink of her ginger beer!

Take a PICNIC CARD from your LUNCHBOX. Now go to 42.

Timmy insisted on sitting at the front of the jeep, wedging himself between Jeff and the commander. 'Right, I believe the ruined castle is north-west of here,' the commander said as he drove quickly through the airfield's gates. 'Perhaps one of you children could find north-west on your compass?'

Use your COMPASS CARD to find north-west by placing it exactly over the shape below – and with pointer touching north. Then go to the number that appears in the window. If you don't have a COMPASS in your RUCKSACK, you'll have to guess which of the numbers to go to.

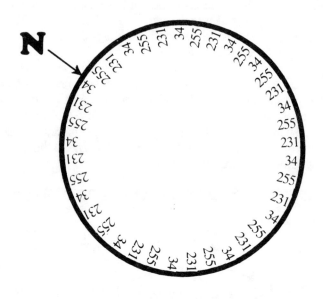

Before anyone had reached for their binoculars, however, George suddenly gave a shout. 'Look, there's the radio mast – right over there!' she exclaimed, pointing into the far distance. 'I just saw its red light flashing.' The others suddenly spotted its flash too and deciding they didn't need their binoculars after all, left them in their rucksacks. They now prepared to set off in the direction of the radio mast but, before they did, Dick insisted on drinking some of his ginger beer. All that running to Toby's farmhouse and back had made him thirsty!

Take a PICNIC CARD from your LUNCHBOX. Now go to 55.

81
By the time they had unstrapped their rucksacks and taken their binoculars out, however, the person on the hill was gone! 'Well, it probably wasn't *us* he was looking at, anyway,' Julian tried to reassure them, as they put their binoculars away again. 'Perhaps it was just a farmer looking for some of his sheep.' But, as they continued on their journey, Julian secretly felt as uneasy about this mysterious watcher as the rest of them! *Go to 274.*

82
They had just located the airfield on their maps when they saw Julian racing back to them. 'I've found something!' he exclaimed excitedly as he squeezed through the hole in the fence again. 'Look – there was this tiny scrap of paper on the floor of the hangar!' He opened it up to reveal a scribbled message inside. It said that the jet was to be hidden at the ruined castle! *Go to 42.*

After walking for a good three-quarters of an hour more, The Five finally reached the airfield. 'Gosh, look how well protected it is!' exclaimed Julian as they peered through a massive barbed-wire fence at the huge airstrip inside. 'We'll have to see if there's an entrance gate somewhere!' So they started to walk along the endless fence, eventually spotting a sentry some distance ahead. They all ran up to him! *Go to 230.*

Just as they were taking out their codebooks, though, Dick noticed that there was a box of matches lying near where the flare had been. Picking them up, he said that Jeff had obviously left both the flare and the matches there deliberately so that anyone coming to rescue him would be able to see where they were going in the cave. They therefore decided to leave the message for the time being, immediately lighting the flare. The prospect of entering the cave did not seem nearly as bad now. Nevertheless, they still had a quick drink of their ginger beer for courage before they did so!

Take a PICNIC CARD from your LUNCHBOX. Now go to 184.

They had only gone a little further when George noticed a map in the grass. On its cover were stamped the letters J.T. 'They're Jeff's initials!' she exclaimed excitedly. 'He must have deliberately dropped this map as he was being taken to the caves. So that proves they *are* this way!'

If you don't already have it, put the MAP into your RUCK-SACK. Now go to 284.

They finally reached the ruined castle, although the commander stopped the jeep a couple of hundred metres short of it so that they were well out of sight. 'I want you all to sit here while I creep up to the castle and check the situation,' he whispered. After a tense five minutes or so, the commander returned to the jeep. 'The jet's still there, thank goodness!' he told them with relief. 'Which obviously means that the two men and the foreign pilot haven't come here yet. We'll just sit here and wait for them!' As they were waiting, the commander showed them a scrap of paper he had found near the jet. There was a coded message on it!

Use your CODEBOOK CARD to find out what the message said by decoding the instruction below. If you don't have a CODEBOOK in your RUCKSACK, go to 119 instead.

When they had found the fork in the track on their maps, they looked up Toby's farmhouse as well so they could work out the distance between the two. 'It's about a mile,' calculated Julian. 'So, since we must have come a good half mile already, we should be there in no more than a quarter of an hour!' On their way to where the track divided, Timmy suddenly started sniffing at something in the grass at the side. 'Look, it's a compass!' George exclaimed after she had gone over to investigate. 'Let's take it with us as a spare!'

If you don't already have it, put the COMPASS CARD into your RUCKSACK. Now go to 55.

'We must be here,' said Dick, pointing to where a copper mine was shown on his map. 'It's the only one in the area.' They then looked to see if Toby's farm was marked as well so they could work out how far they had come. 'Yes, here it is – Gorsehill Farm,' said Julian, indicating with his finger. As they put their maps away again, Anne remarked that it must be nice to live in the middle of the wilds, like Toby. Because there were so few other houses around, it meant your home was bound to be shown on the map! *Go to 57.*

George won the race to the gypsy camp, asking there if they were going the right way for the airfield. 'Yes, you be 'eading straight for it, dearie,' one of them told her. The children were just about to leave the camp when another of the gypsies told them to wait, and went rushing into his caravan. He re-emerged with a pair of binoculars, saying he had found them in the grass nearby. 'They'll likes be very useful to you on your travels,' he told them. 'I'll sells them to you for fifty pence!' Julian was just about to reply that they already had a pair of binoculars each when he noticed a coded message scratched on them. He quickly looked for his codebook!

Use your CODEBOOK CARD to find out what the message said by decoding the instruction below. If you don't have a CODEBOOK in your RUCKSACK, go to 160 instead.

Dick quickly worked out the rest of the message as: *BE AS QUICK AS YOU CAN!* He wondered who had written it but, as he was returning the codebook to his pocket, he suddenly spotted a compass just below the message. He wondered whether that might be a clue and so took it with him as he hurried back to the fence. 'Perhaps there's a name engraved on it!' he told the others hopefully as they began to examine it. Unfortunately, there wasn't – but at least Dick had that message to tell them about!

If you don't already have it, put the COMPASS CARD into your RUCKSACK. Now go to 42.

91

Unfortunately, however, the code on the wire-cutters was different to the one in their codebooks and so they couldn't work it out. They therefore continued along the disused railway line but hadn't gone much further when Julian suddenly tripped on one of the sleepers. The others rushed to help him up, asking if he was all right. '*I* am,' he replied despondently, 'but I don't think my bottle of ginger beer is. I can hear this tinkling sound from my lunchbox!'

Take a PICNIC CARD from your LUNCHBOX. Now go to 116.

92

As they were slipping off their rucksacks to look for their binoculars, however, Dick noticed a little wooden marker at the side of the railway line. Painted on the marker were the words ONE MILE. 'That must mean one mile to the railway's end,' he said, pointing out the marker to the others. 'So we don't need our binoculars to find it after all!' Before continuing along the line, they decided to have a quick drink of their ginger beer. The sun was really quite hot now and they were all feeling rather thirsty!

Take a PICNIC CARD from your LUNCHBOX. Now go to 116.

93

While the children were hurriedly looking for their codebooks, though, Timmy *sat* on the sleeper with the message! He was so pleased with himself at finding it that he forgot what he was doing. Suddenly he realised and quickly jumped up again before the children saw him – but the chalk had all come off on his fur! 'Hey, what's happened to the message!' Dick exclaimed when he was the first ready with his codebook. 'It's suddenly disappeared!' The children simply couldn't understand it but decided they would just have to forget about the message. 'Anyway, here's a piece of cake for being so clever in finding it,' George told Timmy as they now turned to go in the opposite direction along the line. Timmy only hoped that she didn't notice his chalky coat!

Take a *PICNIC CARD* from your *LUNCHBOX*. Now go to 236.

94

George had led them about halfway across the stepping-stones when she suddenly stopped. 'You might give us warning when you're going to stop,' Dick told her crossly from behind. 'You nearly made me fall into the river then!' George replied that she couldn't help it, though – she had suddenly noticed a message chalked on to one of the stones! 'It says: *WHEN YOU REACH THE LAST OF THE STONES, WALK 40 PACES SOUTH-*

EAST,' she told them excitedly. She asked Dick to take the compass from her rucksack so she would have it ready when she came to the last stone!

Use your COMPASS CARD to find south-east by placing it exactly over the shape below – and with pointer touching north. Then go to the number that appears in the window. If you don't have a COMPASS in your RUCKSACK, you'll have to guess which of the numbers to go to.

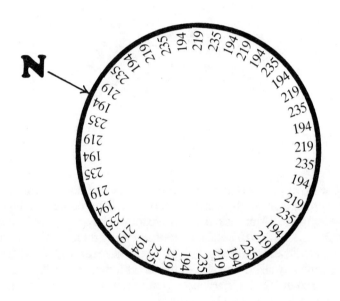

Having worked out the arrow's direction on their compasses, they immediately left the castle. 'I only hope that arrow *did* point to the caves,' George remarked rather anxiously as they hurried along. 'Otherwise, we could be wasting a lot of valuable time!' A short distance further, though, Julian suddenly spotted a shiny brass button in the grass. 'It's an RAF button,' he said excitedly, as he picked it up. 'It must have come from Jeff's jacket. He probably tore it off deliberately to mark the route they were taking!' Since the button proved that they *were* going the right way for the caves, Anne gave everyone a quick drink of her ginger beer to celebrate!

Take a PICNIC CARD from your LUNCHBOX. Now go to 284.

96

The Five eventually arrived at Billycock Caves, finding themselves at two gaping black holes in the side of a hill. 'Are you sure we should enter them?' Anne asked rather anxiously, having noticed a sign that read *DANGER* outside. 'Perhaps we ought to go and inform the airfield and let them search for Jeff?' Julian said there might not be time to walk all the way to the airfield, though – every second could count! So they nervously approached the mouth of one of the caves, waiting to see who would enter first!

Throw THE FAMOUS FIVE DICE to decide.

JULIAN thrown	go to 126
DICK thrown	go to 196
GEORGE thrown	go to 251
ANNE thrown	go to 166
TIMMY thrown	go to 75
MYSTERY thrown	go to 227

'This must be the white cross here,' said Julian when he was the first to find it on his map. 'See? It's a sort of shallow excavation in the hillside. I suppose the pilot is to be dropped there because it would be very easy to spot from the air!' *Go to 252.*

'We're here,' said Anne, when she was the first to find the dug-out cross on her map. 'Can you see? – just above my finger!' They had all put their maps away and were just about to set off again when George noticed a codebook lying in the grass. 'Which silly person nearly left this?' she asked, hoping it was Dick or Julian so she could give one of them a punch! When they checked their rucksacks, however, they all found that they had their codebooks with them. 'It must have been dropped by someone else who came this way!' said Dick mysteriously.

If you don't already have it, put the CODEBOOK CARD into your RUCKSACK. Now go to 163.

George's compass showed that the tunnel was pointing east. When she tried again a few minutes later, it was still pointing east and so it looked as if it *did* lead in a straight line! Just to make sure she waited a while and then read her compass once more. '*Still* east!' she cried joyfully. *Go to 32.*

'Oh no, I think my compass must have dropped out somewhere,' said Julian, tutting with concern as he searched through his rucksack for it. 'I can't find it anywhere!' Much to his relief, though, he finally felt the little metal case – right at the bottom! He now swivelled it round in his hand, trying to locate north-west. *Go to 288.*

Anne went into the front of the jeep, kneeling on the seat so she had a good view. 'Hold tight now,' the commander said as he sped through the airfield gates, 'it's going to be quite a bumpy ride!' To begin with, they went along a small road but then the commander steered the jeep off it and across the rough countryside. He obviously wanted to take as direct a route as possible! Julian noticed that they passed three gigantic stones – two vertical and one flat across the top – and he decided to look them up on his map to find out roughly where they were.

Use your MAP to find which square the stones are in – then follow the instruction. If you don't have a MAP in your RUCKSACK, you'll have to guess which instruction to follow.

If you think A2   go to 202
If you think B2   go to 36
If you think B1   go to 86

102

Anne was still looking for her map when the commander spotted the ruined castle ahead. So she didn't need it after all. The commander stopped the jeep two hundred metres or so short of the castle, well out of sight, while Jeff crept out to check on the situation. 'The jet's still there, fortunately,' he told them with relief when he at last returned to their jeep. 'So the men can't have arrived yet!' While they were waiting for them, Anne passed round the remainder of her cake to relieve the anxiety. They had just finished it all off when a jeep appeared in the distance. As it came nearer, they could just make out two masked men inside – and a third in a flying jacket!

Take a PICNIC CARD from your LUNCHBOX. Now go to 264. (Remember: when there are no picnic cards left in your lunchbox the game is over, and you must start again.)

103

Being the first to find the stones on his map, Dick showed the spot to the others. 'Look, it says they're a prehistoric monument, built in the Stone Age,' he remarked. Just at that moment, Anne returned, telling them that Toby said they had come the wrong way and should head towards the distant radio mast to their left. 'He also gave me this special codebook of Jeff's,' she added as they now set off in that direction. 'He knew we already had codebooks with us but he said this one would probably be a lot better!'

If you don't already have it, put the CODEBOOK CARD into your RUCKSACK. Now go to 130.

104

The Five had left the gypsy camp quite a way behind when Timmy suddenly sniffed out what looked like a small square of card in the grass. 'Oh, leave that alone, Timmy,' George told him. 'It's just a piece of rubbish!' Timmy *wouldn't* leave the piece of card alone, though, insisting on turning it over with his paw. It was then that the children saw that it was a photograph! 'Hey, it's a jet!' George exclaimed as she picked it up. 'And, look, there's some sort of coded message scribbled across it!' So they all quickly slipped off their rucksacks so they could take out their codebooks.

Use your CODEBOOK CARD to find out what the message said by decoding the instruction below. If you don't have a CODEBOOK in your RUCKSACK, go to 40 instead.

They searched every square of their maps for the butterfly farm but they couldn't see it anywhere! 'The farm must be fairly new, built after the maps were printed,' Julian said. They therefore put their maps away again, continuing on their way. Unfortunately, Anne left her compass behind. It had quietly slipped out of her rucksack while she had been putting back her map, and it was lost in the long grass!

If you have it, remove the COMPASS CARD from your RUCKSACK. Now go to 257.

As Anne was making her dash back to the others, however, she suddenly tripped on the concrete! Fortunately, she didn't attract anyone's attention – but she smashed her binoculars in the fall. No time to grieve about it, though. She quickly got to her feet again and continued towards the fence. 'That's the end of my binoculars, I'm afraid,' she panted as she crawled back through the hole. 'Still, there's some good news. I found a message which said that the jet was to be hidden at the ruined castle!'

If you have it, remove the BINOCULARS CARD from your RUCKSACK. Now go to 224.

107

After what had seemed hours of walking, The Five finally reached the ruined castle. 'I've got an awful feeling this has all been a wasted journey,' said Julian as they approached its crumbling walls. 'There obviously isn't a jet anywhere *outside* the castle walls – and I don't see how it could have landed *inside*!' But as they passed through an archway to the area inside the castle, they saw something huge standing there, hidden under a massive green net. Barely able to contain their excitement, they all grabbed hold of one of the net's corners, starting to lift it up! **Go to 253.**

108

While the children were looking for their maps, however, there was a loud screeching noise above. 'It's one of our jets coming down to land!' Jeff cried delightedly as they all stared up at it. 'Look, it's heading in the direction of that radio mast in the distance. So that's the way *we* want to go!' Before they set off, however, Dick gave everyone one of his sandwiches to help fortify them for the long journey!

Take a PICNIC CARD from your LUNCHBOX. Now go to 35.

'Let's try looking through our binoculars,' Julian suddenly suggested after a while, amazed that he hadn't thought of it earlier. 'Perhaps we'll be able to spot the airfield's observation tower or something!' No sooner had he spoken than the others shrugged off their rucksacks, searching for their binoculars!

Use your BINOCULARS CARD to try and spot the airfield by placing it exactly over the shape below – then follow the instruction. If you don't have BINOCULARS in your RUCK-SACK, go to 262 instead.

'I'm afraid we've come completely the wrong way!' Julian told the commander when he had found the reservoir on his map. He passed the map forward to him so he could see for himself. 'Heavens, you're right!' the commander exclaimed. 'Never mind, though, it's just a matter of turning round and heading in the other direction. But you'll have to hold on to your hats because we've got a lot of time to make up!' *Go to 86.*

111

It wasn't long before they arrived at the ruined castle, the commander bringing the jeep to an abrupt halt. 'Phew, we're not too late!' he remarked as they saw the jet was still there. 'We'll park a few hundred metres away so we're well out of sight. Then we'll wait for these two men to come with the foreign pilot – and take them by surprise!' Not long after they had found a good hiding place for the jeep, they heard the sound of another jeep in the distance. The commander quickly asked the children to pass him a pair of binoculars.

*Use your **BINOCULARS CARD** to give the commander a better view of this jeep by placing it exactly over the shape below – then follow the instruction. If you don't have BINOCULARS in your RUCKSACK, go to 37 instead.*

G D B O   A   C   D   E D C T E   F O
E C O   TLN WN   NE S OS   N B
T   F   L HR J   OI U E A   E A R B E
L   N N   F RI   V   N S T   U   L E J

112

'South-east is in *that* direction!' Dick said, pointing to his left as he read his compass. They hadn't walked far in the direction Dick had pointed when they noticed a large square of paper blowing towards them. 'Look, it's a map!' Julian exclaimed, after he had stopped it. 'It's of this area too. Let's take it with us as a spare!'

*If you don't already have it, put the **MAP** into your RUCK-SACK. Now go to 55.*

Julian reached the farmer first, asking whether they were on the right track for the airfield. 'Ay, it be about another three mile,' the farmer replied. 'Jus' keep following your nose!' They hadn't followed their noses far when Timmy started sniffing at a rock, trying to turn it over. 'There must be something underneath!' George said as she bent down to help him. There *was* something underneath – a little notebook containing various sketches of aircraft. And above one of the sketches a coded message was written in black ink! 'Let's take out our codebooks and see if we can work out what it means,' George suggested excitedly.

Use your CODEBOOK CARD to find out what the code said by decoding the instruction below. If you don't have a CODE-BOOK in your RUCKSACK, go to 56 instead.

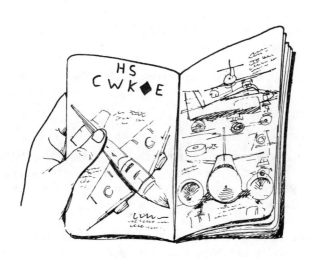

Their compasses showed that the hills – and therefore the airfield – were almost exactly due east. 'Gosh, we *have* strayed a lot,' Julian remarked as they now set off towards the hills. 'The airfield was roughly in a *south*-east direction before that mist came down. The difference between east and south-east is quite a big one!' *Go to 83.*

While the children were busy looking for their binoculars in their rucksacks, however, they heard someone breathing only a few metres away from them! The sound nearly made them all jump out of their skins but, when they looked up to see who it was, they were surprised to find Timmy. He was back at the fence again, crawling through the hole towards them! George noticed that he had a scrap of paper in his mouth and she quickly took it from him. 'Look, there's a message on it,' she exclaimed. 'It says that the jet is to be hidden at the ruined castle. Timmy must have found this on one of the hangar floors!' To reward him for his discovery, she gave him a couple of her meat-paste sandwiches. They were beef-flavoured – Timmy's favourite!

Take a PICNIC CARD from your LUNCHBOX. Now go to 224.

The Five soon arrived at the end of the railway line, finding themselves amongst a few ramshackle sheds. After they'd had a quick look round, Anne suggested looking it up on their maps. It would show them exactly where they were.

Use your MAP to find which square the end of the railway line is in – then follow the instruction. If you don't have a MAP in your RUCKSACK, you'll have to guess which instruction to follow.

If you think D2	go to 107
If you think E3	go to 283
If you think E2	go to 25

'So that's how the hole in the fence got there!' the commander exclaimed when Jeff had at last finished telling him about the two armed men. Rather guiltily, he added, 'And to think we all thought you were a traitor, Jeff! How can you ever forgive us?' *Go to 241.*

'Ah, so that's where we are!' Jeff remarked as Julian showed him the canal lock on his map. 'We're about a couple of miles *west* of the airfield. All we have to do, then, is head east!' George eagerly produced her compass so they could find east but it suddenly slipped out of her hand and rolled towards the canal! 'Oh, what a shame!' Jeff sighed as they watched it disappear into the deep water. 'I was just about to tell you that we didn't need your compass to find east, anyway! According to the map, it's simply a matter of continuing to follow the canal.'

If you have it, remove the COMPASS CARD from your RUCKSACK. Now go to 12.

The children were just looking for their codebooks to decode the message on the scrap of paper when they heard the sound of another jeep in the distance! 'It's coming *this* way!' Jeff exclaimed after they had all listened for a while. 'It must be the one we're waiting for!' He was proved right when the jeep at last came into view. Sitting in the back was a man in a flying jacket – obviously the foreign pilot – and in the front two masked men! **Go to 264.**

120

Anne offered to run back to Toby's farmhouse. She was just about to set off, though, when Julian suddenly had a thought. 'Toby won't be able to tell us which direction to go without knowing roughly where we are,' he said. 'Can anyone see anything distinctive nearby?' Looking round, they spotted three huge stones – two upright and one across the top – a short way to their right and they decided they would probably do. Anne now hurried off, the others sitting down on the grass awaiting her return. They were still waiting twenty minutes later, and so George suggested looking up the three stones on their maps to pass the time.

Do you have a MAP in your RUCKSACK? If so, use it to find which square the stones are in – then follow the instruction. (Remember to put the MAP back in your RUCKSACK afterwards.) If you don't have one, you'll have to guess which instruction to follow.

If you think A2	go to 103
If you think B2	go to 68
If you think C2	go to 263

They were still unstrapping their rucksacks to take out their binoculars, however, when the helicopter suddenly flew off into the distance. 'Well, I don't suppose it was Jeff anyway,' Julian sighed as they continued towards the gypsy camp. 'That theory of mine does sound a bit far-fetched now I think about it. I'm sure if Jeff *had* just had engine trouble, he would have been found long before now!' *Go to 104.*

Their binoculars gave them a good view into the jet's cockpit – but, unfortunately, it *wasn't* Jeff sitting there. This pilot had a moustache, whereas Jeff didn't! They disappointedly returned their binoculars to their rucksacks, and continued their journey. Only a few hundred metres further, however, they stopped again – this time because Julian had spotted a map lying in the grass! 'It must belong to someone at the airfield,' he said, noticing the letters RAF stamped on the cover. 'Let's take it with us so we can hand it in there!'

If you don't already have it, put the MAP into your RUCK-SACK. Now go to 83.

123

'This railway must have been to carry copper from the nearby mines,' Dick said, as he led the way along the disused line. 'The area's much too deserted for it to have been a passenger one.' Anne asked how long they thought the railway line was but no one liked to guess. 'I know what we can do!' exclaimed George, having a quick think about it. 'We can see if we can spot the end of the line through our binoculars. There's bound to be a shed or something there.'

Use your BINOCULARS CARD to try and see the end of the railway line by placing exactly over the shape below – then follow the instruction. If you don't have BINOCULARS in your RUCKSACK, go to 92 instead.

```
  G  B A O   D G H   K LM  T N P  O
R R P T  Z  U W S O       S     R N Q      P E
  M L   T      H S T R N E L W H E F O
 S A F A C   I  D  E  V  F I      L X    E M
```

124

There was such a lovely view from the hill that they thought it would be a nice place to stop and have some of their picnic. 'We can't spend too long, though,' said Julian as he munched into one of Toby's mother's delicious sandwiches. 'We've got to try and find out what happened to Jeff as quickly as possible. Every second wasted is more anguish for poor Toby!'

Take a PICNIC CARD from your LUNCHBOX. Now go to 163.

125

Pointing his compass at the airfield behind them, Dick read its direction as *south-east*. 'Right, so long as we keep remembering south-east,' he told the others as he put his compass away again, 'we should be able to find our way *back* to the airfield!' They had only walked a little further towards the castle when Julian noticed a little book caught in a gorse bush. 'Look, it's a codebook like ours,' he exclaimed as he flicked through the pages. 'In fact it's a lot better than ours, with many more codes. I think we'll take it with us in case it proves useful!'

If you don't already have it, put the CODEBOOK CARD in your RUCKSACK. Now go to 107.

126

Deciding there was no time for nerves, *Julian* entered the cave first. 'Gosh, isn't it dark!' George exclaimed as they all followed him further and further in. 'How are we going to see?' They all felt like kicking themselves for not bringing their torches with them but then Anne noticed a candle and a box of matches on the ground. 'Well spotted, Anne!' Julian remarked as he lit the candle and held it above his head. As the inside of the cave suddenly became much brighter, they noticed that there was a message chalked on the rocky wall! It was in code, though, and so they would have to take out their codebooks.

Use your CODEBOOK CARD to find out what the message said by decoding the instruction below. If you don't have a CODEBOOK in your RUCKSACK, go to 298 instead.

As they were searching through their rucksacks for their binoculars, however, the farmer suddenly attracted their attention. 'Look – there the sock be!' he exclaimed, pointing into the distance. 'The wind couldn't 'ave been blowing before and so it was 'arder to spot.' Before setting off in the direction of the wind-sock, Anne offered the farmer one of her sandwiches for his help. 'That be most kind of you,' he said as he chose a cheese and pickle one. 'Sitting on this tractor all day builds up a real appetite!'

Take a PICNIC CARD from your LUNCHBOX. Now go to 257.

128

They were just about to use their compasses when they heard a slight coughing sound from the left branch of the tunnel. 'It must be Jeff coughing!' Julian exclaimed and they immediately ran down the left branch. The tunnel soon opened out into a small cavern and there on the far side, bound hand and foot, was Jeff! 'Am I glad to see you lot!' he exclaimed with delight as Anne quickly took out her ginger beer to give him a drink.

Take a PICNIC CARD from your LUNCHBOX. Now go to 161. (Remember: when there are no picnic cards left in your lunchbox the game is over, and you must start again.)

129

They were still trying to think how they could find their way back to the airfield, when, all of a sudden, they heard a loud screeching above. Looking up, they saw that it was a jet coming down to land. 'It's going over that way!' exclaimed Jeff, excitedly pointing after it.

'So that must be where the airfield is. Quick, someone take out their compass to check the jet's direction before it disappears!'

Use your COMPASS CARD to find the jet's direction by placing exactly over the shape below – and with pointer touching north. Then go to the number that appears in the window. If you don't have a COMPASS in your RUCKSACK, you'll have to guess which of the numbers to go to.

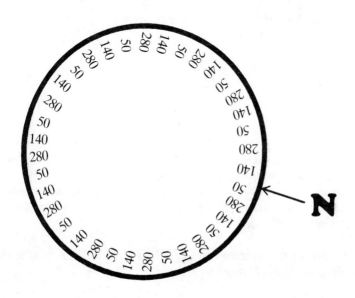

130

After walking for another half hour or so, The Five arrived at an isolated cottage, with a huge glasshouse at its side. To begin with, they thought it was a nursery but then they saw a sign which said BUTTERFLY FARM. Julian suggested they go and see if there was anyone about so they could check they were still going in the right direction for the airfield. As they walked to the back of the glasshouse, two men suddenly appeared. 'What are you kids doing trespassing on our farm?' one of them snarled. They were two of the nastiest-looking men the children had ever seen! *Go to 292.*

131

As soon as they had found the old copper mine on their maps, the children prepared to continue their journey. George forgot to strap up her rucksack again, however, and, as she slung it on to her back, her codebook dropped out. Unfortunately, there was no one standing behind her to spot it. And so it just remained where it was, lost in the long grass!

If you have it, remove the CODEBOOK CARD from your RUCKSACK. Now go to 57.

132

They finally decoded the message as: *THIS IS THE JET WE'RE INTERESTED IN – WE'LL PAY YOU A GOOD PRICE FOR IT!* Julian looked very grave. 'I'm afraid it appears as if Jeff *might* have stolen that jet after all,' he said quietly. 'This is obviously a note from the person who asked him to do it!' Anne still wouldn't believe it, though, saying that the note wasn't necessarily sent to Jeff – it could have been to someone else! 'Well, there's just a slim chance of it, I suppose,' Julian told her doubtfully. He then cheered up a little. 'But just enough for our investigations to continue!' *Go to 83.*

Dick volunteered to go through the hole, taking his codebook with him in his pocket just in case. He certainly wasn't going to take the whole of his rucksack! When the coast seemed clear, he ran across the open concrete towards the nearest hangar. Waiting until he had caught his breath, he slipped inside the hangar, searching round. He was just about to leave and make a run for the next building when he noticed a message chalked on the wall. It began: *JET TO BE HIDDEN AT RUINED CASTLE* – but the rest of it was in code. He excitedly fumbled in his pocket for his codebook!

Use your CODEBOOK CARD to find out what the message said by decoding the instruction below. If you don't have a CODEBOOK in your RUCKSACK, go to 4 instead.

HS ⊗

134

'The castle is roughly north-west,' said Dick, as he read its direction on his compass. 'Right, so all we have to do is make sure we keep going *north-west* through the wood!' They immediately entered the wood, still holding their compasses. It's a good job you thought of this, Dick,' Julian told him as he kept glancing at his compass. 'There are so many paths in this wood that we could well have gone round and round in circles otherwise!' *Go to 163.*

135

'There he is!' Dick exclaimed as he spotted Timmy through his binoculars. 'Right over there – near that clump of trees!' They all shouted at Timmy to wait as they ran after him. 'Fancy leaving us all behind!' George told her dog crossly when they had finally caught him up. 'We couldn't help being so slow crossing the river!' *Go to 181.*

136

'I know what we can do!' exclaimed George suddenly. 'Since the caves are only a couple of miles away, perhaps we could spot them through our binoculars. Let's climb to the top of that tower over there so we get a really good view!' The tower was at one of the castle's corners and it was the only one intact. Luckily, the stone stairway was in fairly good condition and so they reached the top quite safely. As soon as they had done so they quickly unstrapped their rucksacks for their binoculars!

*Use your **BINOCULARS CARD** to try and spot the caves by placing exactly over the shape below – then follow the instruction. If you don't have **BINOCULARS** in your **RUCKSACK**, go to 63 instead.*

```
  G  E  B  O B  C  A A    H  F      T L M  O
W  U O  T S  N    W       E    O           R P
  E  Z S R   I G   M L  X    E  C  H   E H  T
A  C  T  H H  W R          E    O  N  E           L
```

'It must have switched itself on when I kicked it!' Anne remarked gleefully as she picked the bicycle lamp up. She didn't feel quite so nervous now she could see! They all started to wonder where the lamp came from but then Anne noticed a coded message scratched across it. She excitedly told them all to take out their codebooks!

Use your CODEBOOK CARD to find out what the message said by decoding the instruction below. If you don't have a CODEBOOK in your RUCKSACK, go to 260 instead.

138

'There seems to be a small cavern ahead,' Dick remarked tensely as he was the first to find his binoculars, pointing them up the tunnel. 'I can't see anyone there, though . . . Yes, I can! There's a figure huddled against the wall!' Convinced that it was Jeff, he hurriedly led the way towards him. 'It *is* Jeff!' they all exclaimed delightedly as they arrived at the huddled figure. Suddenly recognising The Five, Jeff gave a huge, relieved smile. Although he looked tired and dirty – and he was bound hand and foot – he had obviously never been more relieved! *Go to 161.*

139

'It's obviously the one we're waiting for!' the commander exclaimed after Dick had passed him his binoculars. 'I can see two masked men in the jeep and someone in a flying jacket. He's presumably the foreign pilot!' *Go to 264.*

140

'It's flying east!' George exclaimed when she was the first to find the jet's direction on her compass. As they immediately set off towards the east, Dick asked why they had needed their compasses. 'We could see the jet disappear behind that hill over there,' he remarked bewilderedly. 'Why didn't we just use that as our guide?' As he glanced up at the fading light in the sky, however, he suddenly realised, laughing at himself. It would soon be so dark that the hill would no longer be visible! *Go to 35.*

141

'Look, Toby's written the direction down for us!' Julian exclaimed as he opened the piece of paper Timmy had brought. 'He says we should head for the distant church spire. The airfield is on the way, apparently.' Since they couldn't pick out a church spire anywhere, they immediately went to their rucksacks for their binoculars.

Do you have a BINOCULARS CARD in your RUCKSACK? If so, use it to try and spot the church spire by placing exactly over the shape below – then follow the instruction. (Remember to put the CARD back in your RUCKSACK afterwards.) If you don't have one, go to 175 instead.

```
   G E F O H  H   L   M N  T N P O
  J GT  OLW   NL    J O L E      E D
  T L N S HR  S U W  Y  L  E G O D E
 C  D TH  A       R AW   E   O   E   B
```

The commander was just about to usher them into the jeep when a pilot came rushing towards them. 'Excuse me, sir,' he panted, 'but this parachute was found about a mile away from the airfield. There's some sort of coded message embroidered on it.' Keen to be of help, the children immediately turned to their rucksacks for their codebooks!

Use your CODEBOOK CARD to find out what the message

said by decoding the instruction below. *If you don't have a*
CODEBOOK in your RUCKSACK, go to 243 instead.

143

'Yes, it *is* a parachute!' Dick exclaimed as he focused his binoculars.
Jeff quickly took the binoculars from him, having a look as well. 'It
must be the foreign pilot who's to fly the jet abroad,' he said. 'As
soon as he has landed, I suppose those two men who abducted me
will go to pick him up and transport him to the ruined castle. Let's
just hope we reach it in time!' *Go to 281.*

144

As soon as he had opened his compass, Dick worked out which
direction Toby was pointing. 'It's roughly south-east,' he said.
'That means as long as we keep going south-east, we can't possibly
miss the airfield!' The Five now said goodbye to Toby a second

time, but they had hardly started walking again when Julian spotted a pair of binoculars in the grass. 'I wonder how these got here,' he said curiously, and decided he might as well pop them in his rucksack as a spare. 'You don't think someone's been *spying* on the secret airfield, do you?' he asked as he did so.

If you don't already have it, put the BINOCULARS CARD into your RUCKSACK. Now go to 130.

145

Timmy reached the gypsy camp first but his arrival created such a commotion amongst the chickens there that the gypsies threw a bucket of water at him. 'Take that there dawg away,' one of them shouted at the children, 'or it be an air-pellet he be getting next time!' The children called Timmy to heel, deciding they'd better not ask the gypsies for directions after all! Dick did think of one way in which the gypsy camp could be of use, though. They could look it up on their maps to find out roughly where they were.

Use your MAP to find which square the gypsy camp is in – then follow the instruction. If you don't have a MAP in your RUCKSACK, you'll have to guess which instruction to follow.

If you think C3	go to 159
If you think B3	go to 245
If you think D3	go to 104

146

Their binoculars made all the difference because the yellow wind-sock suddenly came into view, nice and big! As they now continued on their journey towards it, Anne asked what a wind-sock *was*. 'It's to show which direction the wind's blowing,' Julian told her, having learnt about them at school. 'They always have them near the runways on airfields.' *Go to 257.*

They studied their maps for ages but they could see no sign of the airfield. 'Oh, I've just realised why!' Dick exclaimed, tutting. 'Since the airfield's secret, they probably decided not to show it. Otherwise it would be too easy for enemy agents to find it!' *Go to 279.*

'Don't be in such a hurry, Timmy!' George called after her dog rather anxiously as he raced across the stepping-stones. 'You might miss one of the stones and fall into the water!' She gave a sigh of relief as he reached the other bank safely but, by the time George and the others had crossed the stepping-stones themselves, Timmy was gone! 'He must have got fed up waiting for us,' George said, her anxiety rising again. 'Oh, where is he? I can't spot him anywhere!' Nor could the others – and so Dick suggested taking out their binoculars to see if they could help.

Use your BINOCULARS CARD to try and spot Timmy by placing exactly over the shape below – then follow the instruction. If you don't have BINOCULARS in your RUCKSACK, go to 282 instead.

They were still searching for their binoculars in their rucksacks when Julian noticed the cowshed at the side of the farmhouse. 'You don't need your binoculars, after all,' he told the others suddenly. 'It *is* Toby's farmhouse! You remember that Toby's cowshed only had half a roof? Well, look – *that* cowshed only has half a roof as well!' Since Toby was so near, they wondered whether they ought to run across and tell him about their findings so far. But then they decided it would be better to leave it until they knew the full story. So, after having a quick drink of ginger beer to refresh themselves, they continued towards the ruined castle.

Take a PICNIC CARD from your LUNCHBOX. Now go to 107. (Remember: when there are no picnic cards left in your lunchbox the game is over, and you must start again.)

'I was right – the caves *are* shown!' Dick exclaimed, when he won the race to find them on the map. 'Can you see? They're about two miles due south of here.' They were just about to set off in that direction when Timmy found a pair of binoculars near the jet. 'They must be Jeff's!' Julian said, noticing the initials J.T. on them. 'He must have dropped them in the struggle with the two men!'

If you don't already have it, put the BINOCULARS CARD into your RUCKSACK. Now go to 96.

'Has anyone found a compass yet?' George asked as she dug right to the bottom of her rucksack. 'I can't feel mine *anywhere*!' The others weren't having any luck either and Julian was about to suggest that they take their rucksacks back to the outside to do the searching. Suddenly, though, his fingers touched the little metal case – and he quickly pulled it out! *Go to 10.*

152

Their compasses showed that the *left* branch of the tunnel led in a south-east direction and so this was the one they took. The tunnel seemed to be endless but at last it opened out into a small cavern. Peering through the dark, they could just make out a huddled figure at the cavern's far side, bound hand and foot. 'Jeff?' Julian called tentatively, not sure whether the figure was still breathing or not. Jeff took a while to raise his head but, when he did, he gave a huge smile. 'Am I glad to see you lot!' he exclaimed delightedly. *Go to 161.*

153

'Here's the white cross,' Dick told Jeff when he had found it on his map. 'It looks as if it's one of those things that have been carved into the hillside. It would be absolutely perfect for a parachutist to aim for!' When the children had put their maps away again – and Jeff had carefully put the letter away in his pocket for evidence – they all entered the tunnel. They just prayed that it would come out somewhere! *Go to 32.*

As the children were unstrapping their rucksacks for their maps, Anne asked Jeff what a lock was for. 'It's so the canal can go from one level to another,' he told her. 'The water between the gates rises or falls to join the two levels up.' Julian had by now opened his map and was hurriedly searching for the lock. *Go to 118.*

The children immediately checked their watches to find out how long it was to ten o'clock. 'It's just over an hour,' Julian announced – and so they decided they'd better quickly start moving again! 'The fact that that plane circled round a couple of times suggests that it thought *we* were the people to pick up the pilot,' Jeff remarked on the way. 'So perhaps those people are somewhere nearby – watching for the plane.' When, several hundred metres further on, they discovered a pair of binoculars on the ground, it certainly made them wonder!

If you don't already have it, put the BINOCULARS CARD into your RUCKSACK. Now go to 67.

Julian volunteeered to run back to the farmhouse, saying he would be as quick as he could. The others only had to wait fifteen minutes or so before he returned. 'Toby says we should head in a south-easterly direction,' he panted. 'You look through your rucksacks for your compasses while I have a rest!'

Do you have a COMPASS CARD in your RUCKSACK? If so, use it to find south-east by placing exactly over the shape below – and with pointer touching north. Then go to the number that appears in the window. (Remember to put the CARD back in your RUCKSACK afterwards.) If you don't have one, you'll have to guess which of the numbers to go to.

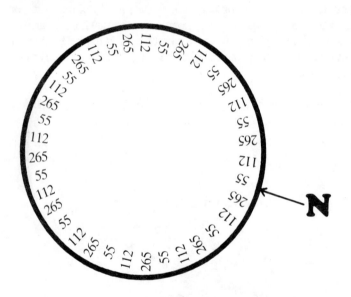

Looking through his binoculars, Julian suddenly spotted the radio mast. 'There it is – right over to the left!' he told the others and they were soon focusing on it too. 'No wonder we couldn't spot it without our binoculars,' remarked Dick as they now set off in its direction. 'It looks absolutely miles away!' They only hoped the airfield would be a lot nearer! ***Go to 55.***

158

The children reached the farmer soon after Timmy, Julian catching his breath before asking if this was the right direction for the airfield. 'Ay!' replied the farmer. 'Jus' keep on going!' So keep on going they did, eventually reaching a derelict stone building with a tall chimney at its side. Julian said it was an old copper mine and suggested looking it up on their maps so they would know exactly where they were.

Use your MAP to find which square the old copper mine is in – then follow the instruction. If you don't have a MAP in your RUCKSACK, you'll have to guess which instruction to follow.

If you think C1	go to 57
If you think D1	go to 131
If you think D2	go to 88

159

As soon as they had found the gypsy camp on their maps, George turned her attention to her dog. 'Poor Timmy,' she said, giving him a hug. 'How cruel that gypsy was to throw water all over you!' Timmy played up to this sympathy, putting on a very sad look for George. In truth, though, he hadn't minded the water one little bit. It had been deliciously cooling! ***Go to 104.***

160

As Julian started to decode the message on the binoculars, however, the gypsy snatched them away from him. 'Me fifty pence first!' he demanded. The children didn't have fifty pence on them, though, and so the gypsy moodily took the binoculars back into his caravan. 'You think he would've at least let me work out the message,' Julian complained as they continued on their way. 'They weren't even his binoculars anyway!' *Go to 274.*

161

Once Timmy had bitten through the thick ropes that bound his hands and feet, Jeff began to relate what had happened to him. 'I was sleeping in my room at the airfield,' he explained quickly, 'when, late in the night, I was woken up by two armed, masked men. They must have got into the airfield by cutting a hole in the fence.' The children realised that that must have been the hole *they* found but they kept quiet, not wishing to interrupt. 'Anyway,' Jeff continued, 'the two men then forced me to walk to the hangar where my jet was kept, saying they wanted me to fly it to the ruined castle. Although I had no choice but to obey, I just had time to leave a message there!' *Go to 62.*

'North-west is over *that* way!' said Julian, stretching out his finger as he read from his compass. The others all followed the direction of his finger, suddenly spotting the tower. It was a small, round brick one, perched on the top of a hill about half a mile away. 'It looks like one of those towers used for lighting beacons on in the old days,' said Julian. 'There are quite a lot of them in this area.' What the others really wanted to know, though, was *who the person was* who was interested in spying on the airfield. And so did Julian, come to that!
Go to 116.

Their journey to the castle at last seemed to be coming to an end, as it grew clearer and clearer ahead. 'I can't *see* any jet there,' said George as they peered at its huge crumbling walls. 'You don't think it was some other ruined castle the message meant, do you?' Dick was still hopeful, though, saying that they might not be near enough yet to see the jet. 'I know,' he suggested, 'let's look at the castle through our binoculars. Perhaps we'll spot something then!'

Use your BINOCULARS CARD to try and find the hidden jet by placing exactly over the shape below – then follow the instruction. If you don't have BINOCULARS in your RUCKSACK, go to 45 instead.

'Yes, I *can* see some white hills!' exclaimed George as she looked through her binoculars. 'They're over there, to the left. Gosh, aren't they strange? They look as if they're covered in snow!' She handed her binoculars to Julian so he could have a look, asking how he thought they became that colour. 'Oh, I know what they are!' replied Julian, after being puzzled by them for a while. 'They're heaps of white waste from a china clay pit. There are meant to be quite a lot of them in this part of the country.' Putting their binoculars away again, they immediately set off towards the white hills. *Go to 96.*

'The arrow's pointing almost exactly due south!' said Julian as they read their compasses. So they immediately set off towards the south, keeping their compasses in their hands. 'I only hope that arrow was scraped by Jeff,' remarked Dick, a little anxiously, as they hurried along, 'otherwise, we could be heading completely the wrong way for the caves!' *Go to 85.*

To begin with, Anne wouldn't have gone first into the cave for all the tea in China. But then she suddenly thought of poor Jeff held prisoner in there and decided there wasn't time to be nervous about it. If no one else would do so, then she would just have to lead the way herself! As it grew darker and darker, however, she could feel her knees tremble like jelly. 'Oh, what's that!' she cried as she nearly tripped over something on the ground. At that very moment, though, a light started to shine at her feet. It was a small bicycle lamp! *Go to 137.*

167
'There's a couple of shadowy figures running away, back towards the entrance!' Dick exclaimed as he pointed his binoculars down the tunnel. 'I wonder what they've been up to?' Timmy was just thinking of chasing after them when there was an enormous explosion from further along the tunnel. The next thing they knew, the tunnel was completely blocked by a massive pile of smoking rocks! *Go to 9.*

168
They had left the bridge quite a way behind when Timmy suddenly stopped in his tracks. He started to sniff at the ground, gradually leading them to several large, flat rocks. 'Timmy's obviously picked up Jeff's scent,' George said proudly. 'He and his two abductors must have stopped for a rest at these rocks!' Examining the rocks,

they suddenly noticed a tiny coded message chalked on one of them. 'It must have been written by Jeff when the two men weren't looking!' Dick said excitedly as they all went for their codebooks.

Use your CODEBOOK CARD to find out what the message said by decoding the instruction below. If you don't have a CODEBOOK in your RUCKSACK, go to 296 instead.

169
'Yes, there *is* a glimmer of light along there!' Dick confirmed delightedly as soon as he had looked through his binoculars. 'In fact, it's more than a glimmer. There seems to be quite a large hole!' He therefore immediately started moving again, happily telling the others that they should be out in the open air in another ten minutes! *Go to 32.*

170
Using Dick's codebook, they all decoded the message as: *THE FOREIGN PILOT WILL ARRIVE BY PARACHUTE. WHEN YOU'VE PICKED HIM UP, TAKE HIM TO THE*

STOLEN JET BY JEEP. 'This must be those two men's instructions,' the commander said thoughtfully. 'Well, if we hear a jeep approaching, we'll know that it's them!' Hardly had he finished speaking than they *did* hear a jeep. Before long they could see it as well! There were two masked men sitting inside and a third in a flying jacket. He was obviously the foreign pilot! *Go to 264.*

171

As George was looking for her compass, though, she suddenly screamed. 'Oh, what's that?' she shrieked, feeling something land in her hair. Jeff plucked it out for her, however, telling her that it was only a leaf. 'And you know what that means, don't you?' he asked, suddenly realising. 'If a leaf has blown in, then the tunnel must have an opening to the outside!' Before they continued up the tunnel, Anne gave everyone a sandwich to celebrate!

Take a PICNIC CARD from your LUNCHBOX. Now go to 32.

172

While they were still looking for their binoculars, however, Jeff suddenly gave a cheer. 'It *is* the airfield!' he exclaimed delightedly. 'Look, the floodlights have just gone on and you can see some of the hangars!' To celebrate, Dick gave everyone a quick drink from his bottle of ginger beer. 'Right, now we've been refreshed,' he said keenly, 'let's *run* the rest of the way!'

Take a PICNIC CARD from your LUNCHBOX. Now go to 67.
(Remember: when there are no picnic cards left in your lunchbox, the game is over and you must start again from the beginning.)

173

Julian climbed into the front of the jeep, the others all quickly piling into the back. Immediately starting the engine, the commander sped through the airfield's gates and out across the rough country-side. They had gone quite a way when Dick spotted a curious white heap on the ground some distance to their right. He quickly searched for his binoculars to find out what it was!

Use your BINOCULARS CARD to obtain a better view of this curious heap by placing exactly over the shape below – then follow the instruction. If you don't have BINOCULARS in your RUCKSACK, go to 220 instead.

174

Julian suddenly realised they didn't need to look up their maps, though, because there *was* the forking of the track, just a short way ahead! As they continued towards it, Dick thought it was now about time for George to hear the truth. 'You're not *half* as fast as us boys,' he told her teasingly, 'and you know it!' George gave him a punch, asking why he hadn't said that before she had run all the way back to the farmhouse. 'Because we didn't feel like going ourselves!' he chuckled, rubbing his arm. *Go to 55.*

175

They were still groping around in their rucksacks for their binoculars when they heard a bell start to ring in the distance. Glancing up to see where it was coming from, they spotted the church spire! 'Oh, it's over *that* way,' Julian exclaimed. 'We've been looking in completely the wrong direction!' Before they set off towards the church spire, George insisted that Dick give Timmy a slice of his cherry cake. 'It's to say you're sorry for calling him daft!' she told him.

Take a PICNIC CARD from your LUNCHBOX. Now go to 130.

They were only about halfway to the gypsy camp when a military
helicopter suddenly appeared, and began to hover just above them.
'I wonder what it's up to?' Julian asked, as they all came to a stop.
'Hey – you don't think it's Jeff up there, do you?' he added
excitedly. 'Perhaps his jet just had some sort of engine trouble and
the helicopter is returning from having picked him up. He might
have recognised us from the air and is trying to tell us that he's all
right!' They shielded their eyes, peering hard at the helicopter's
glass front, but it was too far away. 'I know,' exclaimed Anne
suddenly, 'let's use our binoculars!'

*Use your BINOCULARS CARD to try and see if it is Jeff by
placing exactly over the shape below – then follow the instruction. If you don't have BINOCULARS in your RUCKSACK, go
to 121 instead.*

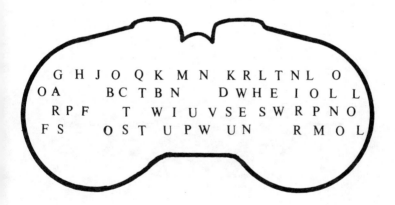

177

'I don't like the look of this,' said Julian, with concern, when he was
the first to work out the coded message in the notebook. 'It says:
SKETCHES OF JETS SEEN AT SECRET AIRFIELD. It
would suggest someone has been observing them illegally!' They all
began to wonder whether that someone was an enemy agent. *Go to
257.*

178

The inscription on the case worked out as: *USE THIS CAMERA TO TAKE PHOTOGRAPHS OF THE JET*. 'I don't like the sound of this,' said Julian with concern as they all put their codebooks away again and continued towards the farmer. 'Someone has obviously been taking secret pictures of one of the jets at the airfield. That could well mean that there are enemy spies in the area!' *Go to 57.*

179

Anne said *she* had better explore the airfield because, being the smallest, she was the least likely to be spotted! So with her heart in her mouth, she crawled through the small hole in the fence and then ran across the concrete towards the shelter of the nearest hangar. She'd decided it would slow her down too much to carry her rucksack but she had her binoculars round her neck just in case. She was just about to peep into the hangar to see if it was empty when she spotted a tiny message chalked to one side. It read: *JET TO BE HIDDEN AT THE RUINED CASTLE*. She immediately made up her mind to run back to the others at the fence so they could see if there was a ruined castle shown on their maps!

Use your MAP to find out which square the ruined castle is in – then follow the instruction. If you don't have a MAP in your RUCKSACK, you'll have to guess which instruction to follow.

If you think A2	go to 224
If you think B1	go to 106
If you think A1	go to 59

180

When they had found the beacon-tower on their maps, Anne asked *why* people used to light beacons. Julian told her that it was an old-fashioned way of signalling important news, like the crowning of a new king or the winning of a great battle. 'There would usually be a chain of beacons,' he told her. 'When you saw one lit in the distance, you would then light your own. That way, the news would pass right through the country!' *Go to 236.*

They hadn't left the river far behind when Julian insisted they all stop for a moment. 'I've just thought of something,' he said. 'If we *do* find the jet hidden at the ruined castle, we'll have to go back to the airfield to tell the commander there. So we'd better all start memorising our route!' Dick said there was a much easier way of finding their way back, though. All they had to do was check the direction of the airfield on their compasses – now, while they could still see it! – and that was the direction they should follow on their return.

Use your COMPASS CARD to read the direction of the airfield by placing exactly over the shape below – and with the pointer touching north. Then go to the number that appears in the window. If you don't have a COMPASS in your RUCKSACK, you'll have to guess which of the numbers to go to.

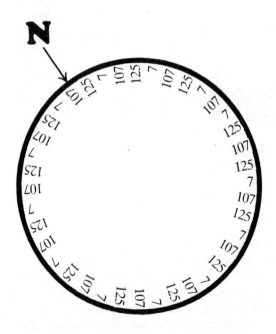

They all held their binoculars to their eyes, slowly looking round. Suddenly, Dick stopped! 'I think I've spotted them!' he cried. 'See that small hill over there? There are two large holes at its base. I bet they're the caves!' When they had focused on the hill as well, the others all agreed with Dick and so they quickly returned to the bottom of the tower in order to set off in that direction! *Go to 96.*

183

'South-east is over in *that* direction!' George said, pointing slightly to her left, when she was the first to have worked it out on her compass. After thanking the shepherd, they now set off that way, keeping their compasses in their hands for a constant check. 'I do hope we're going to be in time,' Julian remarked anxiously as they hurried along. 'Jeff's message made it sound as if his life might be in danger!' *Go to 284.*

184

The children had hoped the cave wouldn't extend very far but it seemed to go on and on, narrowing down to a sort of tunnel. 'Surely it can't go on forever!' Anne remarked anxiously after they'd been following the tunnel for a good quarter of an hour. They had only walked a little further when they suddenly heard what sounded like someone coughing ahead! George was just about to call out, assuming it was Jeff, when Julian stopped her. 'It might be one of his abductors,' he told her cautiously. 'Let's use our binoculars first to see if we can make the person out!'

Use your BINOCULARS CARD to try and see this person by placing exactly over the shape below – then follow the instruction. If you don't have BINOCULARS in your RUCKSACK, go to 208 instead.

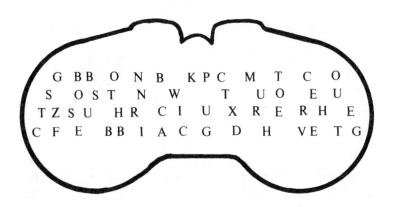

The coded message didn't say where the tunnel came out but it *did* say how much further it had to go. *'END OF TUNNEL IS ANOTHER FOUR HUNDRED METRES,'* Julian decoded delightedly, using Anne's codebook. They had only gone a few of those metres when Jeff spotted an old-fashioned pair of binoculars on the ground. 'They must have belonged to the same person who wrote that message,' he said curiously. 'He must have lived quite a while ago by the look of them!'

If you don't already have it, put the BINOCULARS CARD into your RUCKSACK. Now go to 32.

186

Dick was still trying to find his binoculars in his rucksack when Timmy suddenly dashed ahead, barking excitedly. 'Timmy only makes that sort of bark when he's chasing rabbits!' George exclaimed, laughing. 'That must mean it was just a rabbit that made the noise!' On hearing this, the others all quickened their step, becoming a lot more hopeful. If there was a rabbit in the tunnel, then the tunnel must surely come out somewhere! In his excitement, though, Dick forgot to strap up his rucksack properly . . . and his map quietly slipped to the ground on the way!

If you have it, remove the MAP from your RUCKSACK. Now go to 32.

Anne's map showed that there was only about another mile to the ruined castle from where the road divided. In fact, by the time she had put her map away again, it could be seen ahead! The commander stopped the jeep about two hundred metres short of the castle, well out of sight, telling them all to wait there while he went to check on the situation. After a long, tense wait, he returned to them. 'The jet is still there, thank heavens!' he said. 'Which means that our villains can't have arrived yet.' At that very moment, though, another jeep appeared in the distance. And inside were two masked men and a third in a flying jacket! *Go to 264.*

Having found the stone cross on their maps they were just putting them away again when Anne noticed a codebook near her feet. 'Which careless person has dropped this?' she asked. When they checked their rucksacks, however, they found that they all had their codebooks with them! 'It must have belonged to some other person who came this way,' said Jeff, rather suspiciously, as they picked it up. 'I wonder if it was one of those two men who abducted me? They're more likely than most to have had use for a codebook!'

If you don't already have it, put the CODEBOOK CARD into your RUCKSACK. Now go to 67.

Having found the reservoir on his map, Julian told the commander that he needed to turn round and go in completely the opposite direction! The commander drove so fast, to make up for all the time they had lost, that Dick's lunchbox jogged off the seat, crashing to the jeep's floor. As Dick bent down to pick it up he saw that the lid had come open and most of his remaining sandwiches were now covered in dirt!

Take a PICNIC CARD from your LUNCHBOX. Now go to 86.
(Remember: when there are no picnic cards left in your lunchbox the game has to stop, and you must start again.)

Before the others could stop him, *Timmy* raced back towards Toby's farmhouse. 'What a daft dog you've got, George!' Dick told her. 'I know he'll be a lot quicker than us but how can *he* possibly ask Toby which direction we should go!' Somehow, though, Timmy *had* managed to make Toby understand what they wanted because when he returned he had a piece of paper tucked under his collar! *Go to 141.*

'It's one of those horrible men from the butterfly farm!' Dick exclaimed as they focused their binoculars on the person standing on the hill. Realising this, they all shivered slightly, wondering why he was spying on them. 'Oh, I'm sure he wasn't really spying,' Julian tried to reassure them as they continued on their way. 'He was probably just up there looking for butterflies!' Fortunately, their anxiety was soon forgotten, however, because Timmy suddenly spotted a compass lying in the grass. 'Well done, Timmy!' George cheered as she hugged him round the neck. 'We'll take this with us as a spare!'

If you don't already have it, put the COMPASS CARD into your RUCKSACK. Now go to 274.

They solved a bit of the coded message each, the whole thing finally working out as: *USE THIS FILM TO TAKE PHOTO-GRAPHS OF JETS AT AIRFIELD.* 'There's something I don't like about this,' remarked Julian with concern. 'You're not *meant* to take photographs of secret aircraft. The only people who would do so are enemy spies!' *Go to 57.*

George hadn't led them far along the disused railway line when she noticed some sort of tool between the sleepers. 'It looks like a pair of wire-cutters,' said Julian as he examined it. 'I wonder who left them here? I would have said one of the men who used to do repairs on this railway – but they look much too new. There's not a patch of rust on them!' Turning the wire-cutters over, he suddenly noticed there was a coded inscription scratched on them. He immediately told the others to take out their codebooks!

Use your CODEBOOK CARD to find out what the message said by decoding the instruction below. If you don't have a CODEBOOK in your RUCKSACK, go to 91 instead.

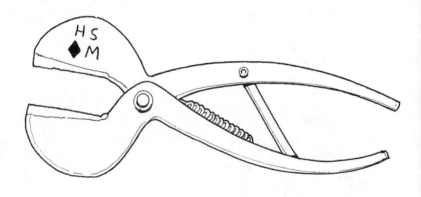

As soon as George had reached the last of the stepping-stones, she found south-east on her compass and then walked the forty paces in that direction. It brought her to a large rock in the grass. Sure that there must be something hidden underneath, she lifted it up. 'Look, a map!' she called back to the others. 'And there's a big cross marked where the airfield is!' They all wondered at the reason for this, finding it rather suspicious. They also wondered for whom the map was intended!

If you don't already have it, put the MAP into your RUCK-SACK. Now go to 163.

195

'The chalked arrow points almost due south,' Julian said when he was the first to find its direction on his compass. As they now quickly set off towards the south, Anne asked why Jeff had just written the *initials* of Billycock Caves above the arrow, and not the full name. 'He probably didn't have time,' answered Dick thoughtfully. 'Don't forget he would've had to have done it very quickly – while the two men who abducted him weren't looking!' *Go to 284.*

196

Dick slowly ventured into the cave first but after only a couple of metres he suddenly stopped. 'How do we know that this is the *right* cave?' he asked over his shoulder. 'It would be a pity to waste our time exploring it if Jeff were in the other one!' He then had an idea. They could peer down this cave with their binoculars. Perhaps they would then be able to spot Jeff. If not, they could try their binoculars at the entrance to the other cave!

*Use your **BINOCULARS CARD** to peer into the cave by placing exactly over the shape below – then follow the instruction. If you don't have **BINOCULARS** in your **RUCKSACK**, go to 47 instead.*

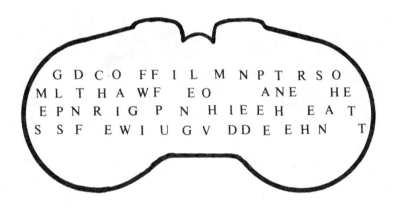

G D C O FF I L M N P T R S O
M L T H A WF   E O   A N E   H E
E P N R I G P N H I E E H   E A T
S S F   E W I U G V DD E E H N   T

197

The coded message clearly *had* been written by Jeff! It worked out as: *ANYONE COMING TO RESCUE ME SHOULD LIGHT THIS FLARE WITH A MATCH. IT WILL HELP YOU SEE WHERE YOU'RE GOING IN THE CAVE.* Fortunately, Julian carried some matches in his rucksack and immediately did as the message instructed, igniting the flare. With this bright light to assist them the prospect of exploring the cave did not seem nearly as bad and so they all now started to enter . . . ***Go to 184.***

Turning round sharply, The Five saw two unpleasant-looking men standing there. 'If you open that door all our butterflies will escape,' one of them snarled. 'What are you kids doing trespassing on our butterfly farm anyway?' Julian put on his politest voice, apologising. 'Oh, I'm sorry, we didn't realise this was a place for breeding butterflies,' he said. 'We thought it was just for growing plants – but I can see all the butterflies now. There are hundreds of them, aren't there? Do you breed them for research?' *Go to 20.*

Dick led them on and on, the tunnel seeming to run for miles. 'Any sign of the end yet, Dick?' Jeff asked after they'd been following it for nearly half an hour. Dick said not but then thought he could see a glimmer of light in the distance. Slipping off his rucksack, he quickly searched it for his binoculars so he could check!

Use your BINOCULARS CARD to see if there is a glimmer of light there by placing exactly over the shape below – then follow the instruction. If you don't have BINOCULARS in your RUCKSACK, go to 13 instead.

The children had a quick look at the container, Julian telling the farmer that it was for a film cartridge. 'Hey, wait a minute,' he added excitedly, prising off the lid, 'there's a roll of paper inside. And, look, there's some sort of coded message written on it!' They all excitedly started to shrug off their rucksacks so they could take out their codebooks!

Use your CODEBOOK CARD to find out what the message said by decoding the instruction below. If you don't have a CODEBOOK in your RUCKSACK, go to 268 instead.

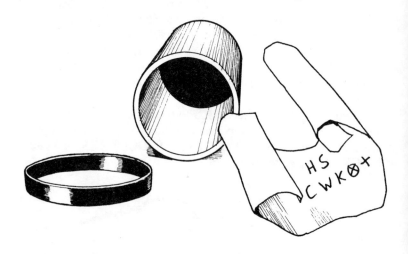

'Oh, we're not as far away from the airfield as I thought!' Jeff remarked joyfully when Anne had shown him the lock on her map. 'It's just a matter of continuing to follow this canal and we should eventually spot the airfield!' As they walked, George asked Jeff why he thought the canal had been built. 'Probably to transport clay from the mines,' he told her. 'There are quite a lot of them in this area.' *Go to 12.*

202

They hadn't gone much further when disaster struck. One of the jeep's tyres suddenly had a puncture! Fortunately, they had a spare, though, and Jeff and the commander quickly jumped out to change it. They had just fixed the spare tyre when Jeff noticed a small book on the ground. 'Why it's a codebook!' he exclaimed, as he quickly flicked through the pages. 'I wouldn't mind betting it was dropped by one of those two men!'

If you don't already have it, put the CODEBOOK CARD into your RUCKSACK. Now go to 86.

203

'Be you looking for somewhere?' the farmer asked from his tractor when Dick reached him. Dick said that they were – the airfield – and enquired whether they were going in the right direction. 'Ay, you be heading straight for it,' the farmer told him, and Dick passed on this good news to the others. Before they went any further, though, Julian suggested they look on their maps for the butterfly farm they had just visited. It would tell them roughly where they were.

Use your MAP to find which square the butterfly farm is in (remember, there was a large glasshouse there) – then follow the instruction. If you don't have a MAP in your RUCKSACK, you'll have to guess which instruction to follow.

If you think D2	go to 105
If you think C2	go to 39
If you think B2	go to 257

204

'North-west is over in that direction,' Dick said, pointing, when George had told the others about the message. Before putting their compasses away again, they tried to work out where five miles would be. 'It's roughly at that ruined castle,' Julian said, squinting at a small hilltop in the far distance. 'The jet must be hidden there!' *Go to 42.*

Not long after they had all followed Dick across the stepping-stones, they reached a gigantic cross cut into the hill. 'We've studied things like this in history,' Julian said as the others all looked rather puzzled by it. 'They were dug out a long, long time ago but no one is quite sure why!' George said that if the excavation was that old, then it was almost bound to be shown on their maps. She therefore suggested looking it up so they would know exactly where they were.

Use your MAP to find which square the excavated cross is in – then follow the instruction. If you don't have a MAP in your RUCKSACK, you'll have to guess which instruction to follow.

If you think C1	go to 98
If you think E1	go to 163
If you think D1	go to 124

Quickly flicking through their codebooks, they decoded the message on the sleeper as: *STEAL THE JET AT ONE O'CLOCK WEDNESDAY MORNING. YOU'RE LESS LIKELY TO BE SEEN AT THAT TIME OF THE NIGHT.* Julian went quite pale, and was not able to speak for a while. 'Wednesday morning was when *Jeff's* jet went missing,' he murmured eventually. 'So it very much looks as if he *was* guilty of stealing it. This message was presumably from the person who gave him his instructions.' Although they continued towards the ruined castle, they felt almost like giving up their investigations. They were afraid of what further evidence they might find against Jeff! *Go to 236.*

207

The children's joy at uncovering the jet was brought to an abrupt end, however. Timmy had found a small diary amongst the grass growing within the castle and on its cover were the words: PILOT OFFICER JEFF THOMAS! 'I'm afraid this confirms beyond all doubt that it *was* Jeff who stole the jet,' Julian began sadly – but when he opened the diary he saw the following message inside: *'I'VE BEEN ABDUCTED BY TWO MEN. I OVERHEARD THEM SAY THEY'RE TAKING ME TO BILLYCOCK CAVES A COUPLE OF MILES AWAY. PLEASE HELP!'* Their spirits suddenly picking up again, the children immediately prepared to set off for Billycock Caves. But where were the caves? They all tried to work out how they could find them.

Throw THE FAMOUS FIVE DICE to decide who is to come up with an idea.

JULIAN thrown	go to 289
DICK thrown	go to 8
GEORGE thrown	go to 136
ANNE thrown	go to 26
TIMMY thrown	go to 259
MYSTERY thrown	go to 46

While they were feeling through their rucksacks for their binoculars, however, the person coughed again. Although the children still
weren't sure whether it was Jeff or not, Timmy was! He suddenly
raced ahead with an excited bark. The children immediately
followed him, soon arriving at a small cavern. There in the corner,
bound hand and foot, was Jeff! 'Am I glad to see you lot!' he
exclaimed with delight as Dick hurriedly took out his bottle of
ginger beer to give him a drink.

**Take a PICNIC CARD from your LUNCHBOX. Now go to
161.** (Remember: when there are no picnic cards left in your
lunchbox the game is over, and you must start again.)

Reading her compass, George told Jeff that the tunnel led in a
north-easterly direction. 'Let me see now,' he considered. 'That
means we're heading towards a flatter part of this area. So the tunnel
will surely have to emerge soon!' George had only led them a little
further along the tunnel when she discovered an old map at her feet.
Since it proved that someone else had once been along there, it made
them even more hopeful!

**If you don't already have it, put the MAP into your RUCK-
SACK. Now go to 32.**

210

It looked as if *Timmy* had suddenly had an idea because he started to bark excitedly. 'What's he trying to tell us?' Jeff asked George bewilderedly. 'His paw seems to be pointing to those white mounds over to our right. They're just waste from a china clay works. How can they help us to find our way?' For a moment George was puzzled by it as well but then she suddenly realised. 'Of course!' she exclaimed. 'Timmy wants us to look up the china clay works on our maps. Then we'll know exactly where we are!'

Use your MAP to find which square the china clay works are in (look for the white mounds!) – then follow the instruction. If you don't have a MAP in your RUCKSACK, you'll have to guess which instruction to follow.

If you think C3	go to 15
If you think B3	go to 108
If you think B4	go to 242

211

The children watched tensely as the commander, Jeff and Timmy went quietly up to the castle themselves, disappearing inside. A few moments later, they could hear several shouts and Timmy's loud, excited barks. 'I wonder what's happened?' Anne said anxiously as it suddenly went quiet again. 'Do you think *our* three have won the fight or those three men?' Her question was soon to be answered, though, because the two masked men now emerged from the castle with their hands pinioned behind their backs by Jeff and the commander! As for the foreign pilot, he was being escorted by a very alert and snarling Timmy! 'We've caught them,' Jeff shouted to the others joyfully. 'Now to remove the masks of these two men and see who they are!'

Use your CODEBOOK CARD to find out by decoding the answer below. If you don't have a CODEBOOK in your RUCKSACK, go to 18 instead.

By the time Dick had found his binoculars, though, whatever it was in the sky had gone! 'The parachute's either reached the ground,' he sighed disappointedly as he started to put his binoculars away again, 'or it wasn't a parachute at all. Now we'll never know!' To make up for his disappointment, he opened his lunchbox and took out a slice of cake. 'Anyone else like a slice?' he asked.

Take a PICNIC CARD from your LUNCHBOX. Now go to 281. (Remember: when there are no picnic cards left in your lunchbox the game is over, and you must start again.)

213

Anne reached the gypsy camp first – but she rather wished she hadn't because she found it a bit scary! 'Oh, don't mind us, ducks!' said a woman in a black shawl, giving her a toothy but kind smile. 'We don't do folks no 'arm. Now what is it you be a-wanting. Directions is it?' This made Anne feel a little more at ease and she politely asked the way to the airfield. 'You 'eads due east from 'ere,' the gypsy woman replied as the rest of The Five arrived. 'Due east and you'll stroll right into it!' The Five therefore took out their compasses to find due east.

Use your COMPASS CARD to find due east yourself by placing exactly over the shape below – then follow the instruction. If you don't have a COMPASS in your RUCKSACK, go to 275 instead.

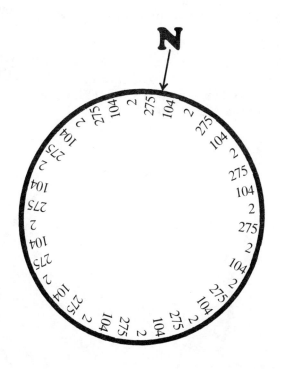

214

Having found east on his compass, Dick waited for the others to arrive. 'What happened to you all?' he asked. 'I thought you were never coming!' Anne explained that they were held up because Timmy had found something in the grass. 'It was a codebook!' she added excitedly, showing it to him.

If you don't already have it, put the CODEBOOK CARD into your RUCKSACK. Now go to 274.

215

Julian had only led them a short way along the railway line when he spotted a message carved into one of the sleepers! It read: *A GOOD PLACE TO SPY ON THE AIRFIELD IS FROM THE TOWER NORTH-WEST OF HERE.* He decided to look up north-west on his compass to see where this good place was!

Use your COMPASS CARD to find north-west by placing exactly over the shape below – and with pointer touching north. Then go to the number that appears in the window. If you don't have a COMPASS in your RUCKSACK, you'll have to guess which of the numbers to go to.

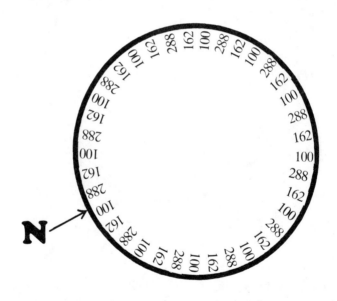

216

Before leaving the shepherd, Anne thought it would be nice to give him a piece of cake for his help. She therefore opened her lunchbox, taking out the biggest slice she had. 'That be mighty kind of you,' the shepherd said as he gratefully accepted it. 'I 'aven't 'ad a bite to eat since me breakfast at five o'clock this morning!'

Take a PICNIC CARD from your LUNCHBOX. Now go to 284.

217

As they started to decode the message, George held the candle so close to the map that it suddenly caught fire! 'Quick, someone try and put it out,' she cried, 'or the message will be lost!' They didn't dare stamp on the map in case they burned their shoes and so Dick swiftly took out his ginger beer bottle and poured some of his drink over the flames. It had been a clever idea but it was too late – the map was now almost completely charred. 'I've wasted a good half of my ginger beer as well!' Dick moaned.

Take a PICNIC CARD from your LUNCHBOX. Now go to 11.

Since she was the most desperate to get out of these horrible caves, Anne led the way along the tunnel! They had followed it for quite a distance when George became worried that the tunnel might not actually be leading anywhere. 'How do we know that it's going in a straight line – and not just round and round in circles?' she asked anxiously. Jeff said she could check by using her compass. If the compass kept showing that the tunnel was pointing in roughly the same direction, then it must be going straight!

Use your COMPASS CARD to check the tunnel's direction by placing exactly over the shape below – and with pointer touching north. Then go to the number that appears in the window. If you don't have a COMPASS in your RUCKSACK, you'll have to guess which of the numbers to go to.

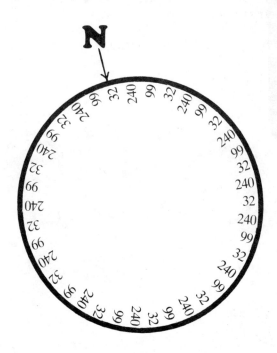

218

By the time George had arrived at the last of the stepping-stones, however, she had forgotten what the message had instructed. So had the others! Did it give the direction as *south*-east or *north*-east, and did it say thirty paces or forty? Julian said he would go back to check but, just as he reached the stone with the message, his lunchbox slipped from his hand. It made such a splash as it hit the water that the chalked message was completely washed off! The river was so deep there that that was the end of his lunchbox as well!

Take a PICNIC CARD from your LUNCHBOX. Now go to 163.

Dick took so long looking for his binoculars, though, that by the time he had found them they were well past the curious heap. He was thinking of asking the commander to drive back to it but then realised how silly the idea was. They couldn't afford a second's delay! *Go to 281.*

221

They were still all trying to persuade each other to do the running back to Toby's farmhouse when they suddenly heard his voice! 'Hey, wait a minute,' he shouted as he came hurrying after them. 'I've just realised that you don't know where the airfield is!' The Five all had a good chuckle at this, telling Toby that they had just realised that themselves! 'Anyway,' Toby said, chuckling slightly himself as he pointed into the distance, 'you want to head in *that* direction.' Dick thought it would be a good idea to work out this direction on a compass and so he started to look for his in his rucksack.

Do you have a COMPASS CARD in your RUCKSACK? If so, use it to take a compass reading of where Toby was pointing by placing exactly over the shape below – and with pointer touching north. Then go to the number that appears in the window. (Remember to put the CARD back in your RUCKSACK afterwards). If you don't have one, you'll have to guess which of the numbers to go to.

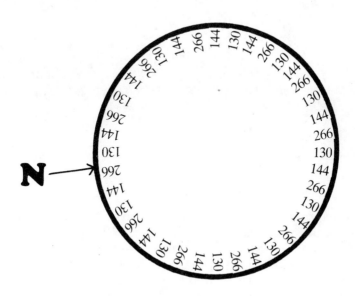

Peering through their binoculars, they saw that it *wasn't* Jeff up there! 'The helicopter must be searching for him in case there's a chance that he crashed somewhere,' Julian guessed. 'Perhaps *they* find it hard to believe that Jeff is a traitor as well!' They now continued towards the gypsy camp but before they reached it they all stopped a second time. This was because Anne suddenly spotted a map lying in the long grass. They decided to take it with them as a spare!

If you don't already have it, put the MAP into your RUCK-SACK. Now go to 104.

When they were all ready with their codebooks, however, Julian suddenly noticed that the inscription was gone! 'It just seems to have disappeared!' he remarked with disbelief as he turned the leather case over and over, this way and that. Then he spotted some white flaky stuff on his fingers. 'Oh no, the paint must have cracked off as I was handling it!' he explained, tutting. That wasn't their only misfortune because, as they continued towards the farmer, it was without Anne's compass. It had quietly dropped out of her rucksack while she had been digging for her codebook!

If you have it, remove the COMPASS CARD from your RUCKSACK. Now go to 57.

224

The Five could just make out a ruined castle on a hill in the far distance and they now set off towards it, assuming it was the one that the message referred to. Or, rather, hoping it was! They didn't really know what the message meant about the jet being *hidden* there but they thought that if they went to the castle, this whole mystery of Jeff's disappearance might become a little clearer. They had walked a good mile on the way to the castle when their path was blocked by a small river flowing down the side of the hill. They therefore went to where there were some stepping-stones, preparing to cross.

Throw THE FAMOUS FIVE DICE to decide who is to cross the stepping-stones first.

JULIAN thrown	go to 248
DICK thrown	go to 205
GEORGE thrown	go to 94
ANNE thrown	go to 299
TIMMY thrown	go to 148
MYSTERY thrown	go to 278

225

'Yes, I *can* see a shed!' Anne exclaimed as she was the first to look through her binoculars, directing them up the line. 'In fact, there are several sheds there – and some buffers. It *must* be the end of the line!' The others now focused on the sheds as well, Dick saying that they were about a mile away. So as soon as they had put their binoculars back in their rucksacks they started walking. ***Go to 116.***

226

Looking through their binoculars, they still couldn't see a jet at the ruined castle, however. 'The message must have meant another one then!' George exclaimed with annoyance. Dick said that the jet might be concealed *behind* the castle, though, and suggested they continue towards it. 'Since we have come this far, we might as well!' he remarked as he led the way. ***Go to 107.***

They were still hesitating outside the cave when Julian spotted a long tubular thing on the ground. 'Look, it's a flare!' he exclaimed, picking it up. 'It must have been dropped by Jeff. Pilots often carry flares with them in case they crash somewhere remote and need to send out a signal.' As Julian twisted the flare round he noticed that there was a coded message pencilled along it. Realising that it had almost certainly been written by Jeff, the children started looking for their codebooks!

Use your CODEBOOK CARD to find out what the message said by decoding the instruction below. If you don't have a CODEBOOK in your RUCKSACK, go to 84 instead.

Ten minutes or so later, The Five at last reached Billycock Caves. They consisted of two gaping black holes in the side of a hill. The Five ventured nervously inside one of them, keeping close together. They hoped that the cave wouldn't extend very far but it seemed to go on and on, narrowing down to a sort of tunnel. Finally, the tunnel opened out again into a small cavern. A sudden coughing sound from the far end nearly made them jump out of their skins! 'Jeff?' Julian asked tentatively as they could just make out a huddled figure there, bound hand and foot. The figure lifted its head, giving a broad smile. 'Am I glad to see you lot!' Jeff exclaimed delightedly. *Go to 161.*

229

'It's just a rabbit!' Dick laughed as he pointed his binoculars along the tunnel. 'I'm afraid Timmy's never going to catch it, though. In fact, he's now given up and is making his way back to us. And a right sorry sight he looks too!' As Timmy trotted back, Jeff suddenly realised something. The only way a rabbit could be in the tunnel was if the tunnel had an opening to the outside! 'I just hope that the opening's big enough!' he added cautiously as he told the others the good news. *Go to 32.*

230

Julian asked the sentry for permission to be let in to see the airfield's commander, saying it was very important. 'It's to do with that stolen jet,' he told him. The sentry became very attentive at this, asking eagerly if they had any more information about it. When Julian replied that they really wanted to do some investigating into the incident, however, the sentry started laughing at them. 'We're perfectly capable of doing our own investigating, thank you very much,' he chuckled. 'Now why don't you kids run off and find somewhere else to play?' *Go to 6.*

231
The children quickly found north-west on their compasses, telling the commander that it was roughly in the direction of the moon. 'It's a good job these jeeps don't have to keep to roads, isn't it?' Dick remarked as they bumped over the rough countryside. 'It means we can take the most direct route!' As the jeep tossed them up and down, George noticed a pair of binoculars sliding along the floor. 'They must belong to one of my men,' the commander said when she told him about them. 'Look after them, will you, George? They might well prove useful!'

If you don't already have it, put the BINOCULARS CARD into your RUCKSACK. Now go to 111.

'Ah, there it is – over there!' Julian said, suddenly spotting the church spire through his binoculars. As they set off towards it, Anne asked why they weren't able to see the airfield too, since it was meant to be on the way. 'It's likely to be hidden between the hills,' he told her. 'Don't forget, an airstrip has to be nice and flat so it's easy for the planes to land.' *Go to 130.*

'Look, what's that behind?' George suddenly screamed when they were all about halfway to the farmer. Everyone stopped in their tracks to see what it was – but George kept running. It had all been a trick to make sure she reached the farmer first! When she asked the farmer if they were going in the right direction for the airfield, he nodded his head. 'In fact, if you peers 'ard,' he added, 'you should be able to see its yella wind-sock.' George and the others did peer hard but without any luck. 'I know – let's try looking through our binoculars!' suggested Dick.

*Use your **BINOCULARS CARD** to try and locate the wind-sock by placing exactly over the shape below. If you don't have **BINOCULARS** in your **RUCKSACK**, go to 127 instead.*

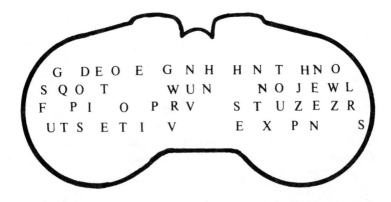

As George was leaving the hangar, though, she suddenly discovered another chalked message. This time it was on the wall near the entrance. It read: *FIVE MILES NORTH-WEST IS THE RUINED CASTLE*. So we won't be needing our compasses after all, she thought as she hurried back to the others at the fence. Before telling them about the two strange messages, however, she insisted on having a long drink of her ginger beer. All that running had made her hot!

Take a PICNIC CARD from your LUNCHBOX. Now go to 42.

As Dick was reaching into George's rucksack for her compass, however, he suddenly slipped from his stepping-stone! Although he managed to avoid falling right into the river, it still came all the way up to his knees. 'Ugh, my trousers are soaking!' he cried. All the others were concerned about though was the chalked message. The large splash Dick had made had completely washed it off – and no one could remember what it had said! George had extra reason to be annoyed. Dick had knocked her map from her rucksack when he slipped and it was now rapidly disintegrating in the water!

If you have it, remove the MAP from your RUCKSACK. Now go to 163.

The Five had travelled a good deal closer to the ruined castle when they spotted a small farmhouse across the valley. 'That looks a bit like *Toby's* farmhouse!' Anne exclaimed, peering at it. 'It has two chimneys like his and it's the same grey colour. Do you think we're back near the place we started from?' Julian thought it looked very much like Toby's farmhouse, too, but George said there were lots of farmhouses of that colour and with two chimneys. 'Well, there's only one way to make sure,' Dick said, suddenly having an idea. 'Let's look at it through our binoculars!'

Use your BINOCULARS CARD to obtain a clearer view of the farmhouse by placing exactly over the shape below – then follow the instruction. If you don't have BINOCULARS in your RUCKSACK, go to 149 instead.

```
   G  A B O B  K D H  D  M    T P R O
 O H T M L   M N    O W S E    O V T
   I T W  F O   H F  E E   D  U A C A   R
 F H N H M  I Z V  N  P P   E  L  F        E
```

Having found on their compasses which way the chalked arrow was pointing, they now prepared to set off in that direction. George was just heaving her rucksack back on her shoulders, however, when she suddenly noticed Timmy investigating a deep hole in the ground. It was the castle well! 'Timmy, come away from there,' she screamed as she ran over to him. 'If you fall in, we'd never get you back again!' As she yanked Timmy away from the well, however, her rucksack suddenly slipped down to her waist. As it did so, her map fell out, disappearing down the well!

If you have it, remove the MAP from your RUCKSACK. Now go to 284.

238

George had just started searching in her rucksack for her compass when they heard a faint whistling sound ahead. 'Ooh, what's that?' Anne asked, turning white as a sheet. 'You don't think this tunnel's haunted, do you?' Jeff gave a kindly chuckle, however, telling her that it was just the wind. 'And you know what that means, don't you?' he added cheerfully. 'It means that the tunnel must have an exit!' *Go to 32.*

As they were taking their compasses out, however, they suddenly noticed Timmy sniffing towards the left branch of the tunnel. 'He must have picked up Jeff's scent!' George exclaimed excitedly – and they all started to follow him. Timmy went faster and faster along the tunnel, finally bringing them to a small cavern. Peering through the dark to the cavern's far side, they saw that there was a huddled figure there, bound hand and foot. 'Jeff!' they all cried delightedly as the figure slowly raised its head, giving a huge relieved smile. They ran over to him, Anne quickly taking out her ginger beer to give him a drink!

Take a PICNIC CARD from your LUNCHBOX. Now go to 161. (Remember: when there are no picnic cards left in your lunchbox the game is over, and you must start again.)

George was just about to take out her compass when Anne noticed a large sheet of paper at her feet. 'It's an old map of the area,' she exclaimed as she examined it. 'That means someone else must have once been along this tunnel!' More importantly, though, it also suggested that the tunnel must have an exit!

If you don't already have it, put the MAP into your RUCK-SACK. Now go to 32.

Jeff said there was no need for an apology, though. Nor time either–
they had to get to the ruined castle as quickly as possible, before this
foreign pilot arrived to fly the jet abroad. The commander fully
agreed, immediately ordering a jeep to be brought to the door of his
office. As soon as the jeep had arrived, the commander asked The
Five if they would all come along as well. 'Four of you can sit in the
back,' he said as they all went out to it, 'and the other one can sit in
the front with Jeff and me!'

*Throw THE FAMOUS FIVE DICE to decide the one who is to
sit in the front.*

JULIAN thrown	go to 173
DICK thrown	go to 53
GEORGE thrown	go to 17
ANNE thrown	go to 101
TIMMY thrown	go to 79
MYSTERY thrown	go to 142

242

'Ah, so that's where we are!' Jeff remarked when Julian had showed
him the china clay works on his map. 'We need to walk about two or
three miles east from here.' So they immediately set off in an easterly
direction, hoping they would reach the airfield before it became too
dark! *Go to 35.*

243

The commander quickly helped The Five into the jeep, though, saying they could decode the message on the parachute later. 'We must start out for the ruined castle without a moment's delay,' he told them as he switched on the jeep's engine. 'It's most important that we stop that jet being flown abroad!' As the jeep sped out of the airfield, Anne passed round the remainder of her sandwiches. This might be their last chance to eat for a while!

Take a PICNIC CARD from your LUNCHBOX. Now go to 111. (Remember: when there are no picnic cards left in your lunchbox the game has to stop, and you must start again.)

Since it was his idea, Dick offered to run back to the farmhouse himself. He seemed to take ages but eventually he returned with what they wanted to know. 'Toby says we should head in the direction of the tall radio mast in the distance,' he panted. 'The airfield is on the way, apparently!' They immediately started to scan the horizon for a radio mast but they couldn't find one. 'Perhaps we'll have more success with our binoculars,' suggested Anne and they all opened their rucksacks to take them out.

Do you have a BINOCULARS CARD in your RUCKSACK? If so, use it to try and spot the radio mast by placing exactly over the shape below – then follow the instruction. (Remember to put the CARD back in your RUCKSACK afterwards.) If you don't have one, go to 80 instead.

```
G  D E O     E H  L MM    N T  R H O
 H H O  T K N I W      E       B O  E A D
 F Y S S I V U E R V N  E      I N H E
 N   S  I L E    N V L G E      C C  N A
```

While they were taking out their maps, however, the gypsy who had thrown the water at Timmy came running after them! 'I thought I telled you lot to clear orf,' he shouted, brandishing an air-rifle. 'Now you and that dawg be on your ways!' The Five quickly broke into a run themselves, George being in such a panic that she cut right across Julian's path, tripping him up. As he dusted himself down, Julian was relieved to see that the gypsy had finally given up the chase, turning back to his camp. The bad news, though, was that there was a rattle of glass from his rucksack. He must have smashed his binoculars when he fell!

If you have it, remove the BINOCULARS CARD from your RUCKSACK. Now go to 104.

246

They were only about halfway to the farmer when Julian suddenly stopped in his tracks, making them all bump into him. 'Look, someone's dropped a leather camera case in the grass!' he exclaimed, bending down to pick it up. Turning the case over in his hands, he saw that there was a small inscription painted on it. It was in some sort of code, though, and so they were only going to find out what it meant with the help of their codebooks!

Use your CODEBOOK CARD to find out what the inscription said by decoding the instruction below. If you don't have a CODEBOOK in your RUCKSACK, go to 223 instead.

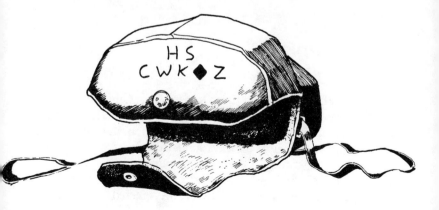

247

As Dick was still looking for his compass, though, the jeep suddenly stopped and reversed back to him. 'I'm awfully sorry,' the pilot told him. 'I've just realised that *east* probably doesn't mean much to you. We pilots are so used to talking compass directions that we forget that other people might be confused by them!' He then stretched out his arm, pointing towards some hills in the distance. 'The airfield is over *that* way!' he said. ***Go to 274.***

248

After they had all followed Julian across the river, they soon arrived at the edge of a large wood. They couldn't decide whether to enter or not. As long as they went in the right direction, it would be a lot quicker than walking all the way round. But, since the ruined castle would no longer be visible once they were inside the wood, how could they be sure they *were* going in the right direction? Suddenly, though, Dick had a brainwave. Before they entered the wood, they could check the castle's direction on their compasses. They would then know which way to go even when they could no longer see it!

Use your COMPASS CARD to find the ruined castle's direction by placing exactly over the shape below – and with pointer touching north. Then go to the number that appears in the window. If you don't have a COMPASS in your RUCKSACK, you'll have to guess which of the numbers to go to.

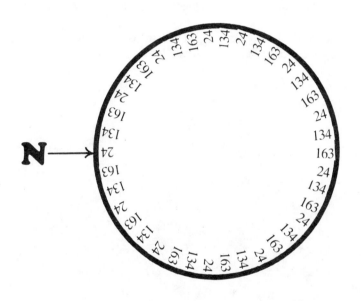

249

'I was right – it *is* Toby's farmhouse!' Anne exclaimed as they all pointed their binoculars across the valley. 'Look, you can just about see Toby himself, walking over to the cowshed!' They wondered whether one of them should run across and tell Toby about what they had learnt so far. But then they decided it would waste too much time . . . and it would be better to leave it until they had found out the full story anyway! ***Go to 107.***

250

The coded message worked out as: *THE TWO MEN HAVE DECIDED TO STOP HERE FOR A SHORT REST. I HEARD ONE OF THEM SAY THE CAVES ARE ANOTHER QUARTER OF A MILE*. The children were eagerly putting their codebooks away again, about to travel this last quarter of a mile, when Julian spotted a pair of binoculars near the rocks. 'I bet they're Jeff's!' he exclaimed as he picked them up. 'Look, they've got RAF engraved on them. He must have left them here deliberately as another clue to the route he was being taken!'

If you don't already have it, put the BINOCULARS CARD into your RUCKSACK. Now go to 228.

251

Realising there was no time to waste, *George* suddenly led the way into the cave. 'I've just thought of something!' she remarked nervously as the cave grew darker and darker. 'How are we going to see? We forgot to bring our torches!' She had only gone a few steps more, however, when she just happened to spot a candle and box of matches near her feet! As she lit the candle, the cave immediately became much brighter and she soon spotted a map on the ground as well. 'Look, there's a coded message written across its cover!' she exclaimed on picking it up.

Use your CODEBOOK CARD to find out what the message

said by decoding the instruction below. If you don't have a CODEBOOK in your RUCKSACK, go to 217.

252

They all now entered the tunnel, praying that it would come out somewhere. The tunnel's floor was quite damp and so they had to be careful they didn't slip. Suddenly George did slip, however, falling flat on her back. Fortunately, her rucksack cushioned her fall but, as she stood up again, she heard a tinkling sound from inside. 'Oh no,' she whined, 'my binoculars must have broken!'

If you have it, remove the BINOCULARS CARD from your RUCKSACK. Now go to 32.

Although it could hardly be anything *but* the jet hidden under the vast area of green netting, it still made them gasp when they saw it. 'So it *did* manage to land inside the castle!' Julian exclaimed as they revealed the tip of one of its wings. 'It must be one of those that can land vertically. I say, how brilliant to think of hiding the jet here! There's no way it can be seen from outside the castle walls and this green net makes sure that it can't easily be spotted from the air either. It would just blend in with all the grass!' *Go to 207.*

'I hope we reach the airfield *soon*,' Julian remarked rather anxiously, after they'd been walking for nearly an hour. 'It's growing darker by the second!' They hadn't walked much further when they spotted a large stone cross on a hill to their right. Julian suggested they look it up on their maps to find out roughly where they were.

Use your MAP to find which square the stone cross is in – then follow the instruction. If you don't have a MAP in your RUCKSACK, you'll have to guess which instruction to follow.

If you think E4	go to 31
If you think C4	go to 67
If you think D4	go to 188

As the children were taking out their compasses, though, the commander suddenly realised that he didn't need them. 'Of course, I can work out north-west from the stars!' he exclaimed, chuckling to himself. 'That's how we used to have to do it when I was a young pilot!' *Go to 111.*

Pointing his binoculars at the curious white heap, Dick saw that it was a parachute! As soon as the commander was told of this, he made a sharp turn, driving the jeep towards it. 'This is a foreign type

of parachute,' he said soberly as he examined it, 'and so it almost certainly belongs to that pilot who's to fly the jet abroad. He must have been dropped from a plane and has since been picked up by those two men. Which means we don't have much time!' Just as they were all about to jump back into the jeep, however, Julian noticed a codebook near the parachute. The commander asked him to put it into his rucksack for them to examine later!

If you don't already have it, put the CODEBOOK CARD into your RUCKSACK. Now go to 281.

257

It didn't take much more walking before the airfield became quite clear in the distance. It was then that a sudden mist descended, however! Only half an hour later it had lifted again but, instead of stopping where they were, The Five had made the mistake of continuing to move. As a result, they had completely lost sight of the airfield! 'Look, it must be somewhere behind those hills over there,' said George, suddenly spotting a jet taking off from that direction. 'Let's take a compass reading on them in case there's another mist!'

Use your COMPASS CARD to find out in which direction the hills are by placing exactly over the shape below – and with pointer touching north. Then go to the number that appears in the window. If you don't have a COMPASS in your RUCK-SACK, you'll have to guess which of the numbers to go to.

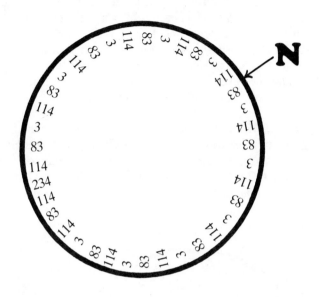

258

They had walked quite a way from the end of the railway line when Dick asked if they could all stop for a moment. Something in his rucksack was prodding into his back and he wanted to repack it. 'Ah, that's what it was – my binoculars!' he exclaimed as, digging inside his rucksack, he found the culprit. He was turning his binoculars round a bit when he noticed that his compass wasn't there. 'Oh, what a nuisance!' he sighed. 'It must have slipped out back at the railway terminus while I was taking out my map. I suppose it's much too far for us to go back for it?' The others agreed – *it was!*

If you have it, remove the COMPASS CARD from your RUCKSACK. Now go to 236.

'It looks as if Timmy has thought of something!' Anne exclaimed with laughter as he suddenly bounded out of the castle, leaving them no choice but to follow. For a long while they wondered where he was leading them but then they spotted a shepherd rounding up his sheep on a neighbouring hill. 'Timmy obviously wants us to ask *him* the way to the caves,' George panted. 'Isn't he clever? He must have heard the shepherd using his sheepdog whistle when we were at the castle!' The shepherd proved very friendly and helpful, telling the children that the caves were in a south-easterly direction. They immediately looked for south-east on their compasses!

Use your COMPASS CARD to find south-east yourself by placing exactly over the shape below – and with pointer touching north. Then go to the number that appears in the window. If you don't have a COMPASS in your RUCKSACK, you'll have to guess which of the numbers to go to.

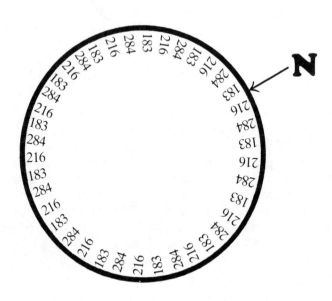

260

They were just about to start looking for their codebooks when
George stopped them. 'We can work out the coded message when
we're outside again,' she told them. 'If we do it now, we'll just waste
the lamp's batteries. It would be much more sensible to keep them
for finding our way!' The others all agreed with her – especially since
they didn't know how much longer the batteries might last – and so
they immediately started moving again. They had only gone a little
way further, however, when Dick, tripping over Timmy, went
crashing to the ground. Although he wasn't hurt, he heard the
sound of tinkling glass in his rucksack as he stood up again. His
binoculars were obviously broken!

*If you have it, remove the BINOCULARS CARD from your
RUCKSACK. Now go to 184.*

261

Julian had led them all quite a way along the narrow tunnel when he
suddenly spotted a message chalked on its roof. Unfortunately, it
was in code, however, and so he turned round to ask one of the
others to hand him a codebook. 'Perhaps it says where the tunnel
comes out,' he remarked excitedly.

Use your CODEBOOK CARD to find out what the message

said by decoding the instruction below. If you don't have a
***CODEBOOK** in your **RUCKSACK**, go to 76 instead.*

262

'Your binoculars won't be necessary after all!' Jeff suddenly exclaimed while the children were still searching for them in their rucksacks. 'Look, *there's* the observation tower in the distance! They've just this moment switched its lights on!' The tall, illuminated building looked about three or four miles away and so Dick gave them all a drink of his ginger beer before they started the long journey. He pretended he was just being generous but the *real* reason behind it was to make his lunchbox easier to carry!

*Take a **PICNIC CARD** from your **LUNCHBOX**. Now go to 254.*

While they were searching through their rucksacks for their maps, Dick asked Julian what he thought the stones were. 'Someone must have put them like that,' he said. 'There's no other way that one across the top could have got there!' Remembering a history lesson he had had at school, Julian replied that Dick was quite right – someone *had* put them like that. It was people in the Stone Age! *Go to 68.*

The other jeep came nearer and nearer, suddenly switching off its lights and driving the last part of the way by moonlight. 'Phew, that's a relief!' Julian whispered as they all anxiously watched. 'I was worried that their headlights might show us up.' The men obviously didn't see them, though, steering their jeep right up to the castle walls. 'I want you children to stay here in case the men are still armed,' the commander whispered as they saw the two entering the castle. 'Jeff and Timmy – you come with me!' *Go to 211.*

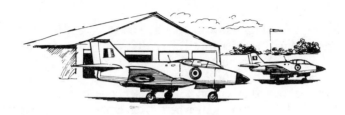

265

While they were opening their rucksacks to take out their compasses, however, they saw a jet coming down to land in the distance. 'The airfield must be over in that direction then!' Dick remarked. 'We don't need to use our compasses after all!' So they all strapped their rucksacks up again, heaving them on to their backs ready to start moving. *Go to 55.*

266

The Five now said goodbye to Toby a second time, and began their journey again. 'I wonder why Toby didn't want to come with us?' Anne asked. 'You would think he would be keen to do some investigating at the airfield himself.' Julian said it was probably because he wanted to remain near the telephone in case his cousin Jeff suddenly rang from somewhere. 'Remember, Toby's parents are out at the moment,' he added, 'and so he's the only one there to answer a call.' *Go to 130.*

Dick reached the gypsy camp first, but, just as he did so, he noticed a military jeep coming in the other direction along the track. Inside was a pilot and so he decided to ask him the way to the airfield instead. It was probably where he had just driven from! 'You want the airfield, eh?' said the pilot when Dick had hailed his jeep. 'Well, it's exactly due east from here. But if it's a look round you're after, I'm afraid you're going to be disappointed. The place is top secret!' As he drove off, Dick searched through his rucksack for his compass so he could find out where east was.

Use your COMPASS CARD to find east yourself by placing exactly over the shape below – and with pointer touching north. Then go to the number that appears in the window. If you don't have a COMPASS in your RUCKSACK, you'll have to guess which of the numbers to go to.

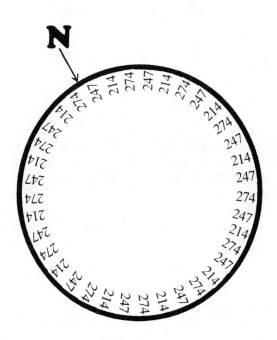

Before Julian could slip off his rucksack, though, a gust of wind came up and snatched the scrap of paper out of his hand! He chased after it as it blew up into the air, his rucksack half off his shoulders. The rucksack proved such an encumbrance, however, that he lost his balance and fell flat on his back. By the time he was up again, the scrap of paper was far away in the distance and impossible to catch. There was even worse news. He had fallen so heavily that the glass in his binoculars had shattered. They were now completely useless!

If you have it, remove the BINOCULARS CARD from your RUCKSACK. Now go to 57.

269

They finally decoded the message on the scrap of paper as: *JET IS TO BE HIDDEN AT THE RUINED CASTLE. I'VE WRITTEN THIS IN CODE SO THE VILLAINS WON'T REALISE WHAT IT'S ABOUT IF THEY FIND IT.* Although the children didn't have a clue who could have scribbled the note, they could see that it was obviously very important! *Go to 224.*

270

Anne led the way along the disused railway line, treading from sleeper to sleeper. It wasn't long, though, before the railway line came to an end and they were walking across normal ground again. Passing the bottom of a hill, they noticed an odd-shaped stone tower at the top. Julian said that it was probably one of those towers that was used for lighting beacons on in the old days. He then suggested looking it up on their maps to find out their position.

Use your MAP to find which square the beacon-tower is in – then follow the instruction. If you don't have a MAP in your RUCKSACK, you'll have to guess which instruction to follow.

If you think E1	go to 180
If you think D1	go to 23
If you think D2	go to 236

271

They were putting their maps back in their rucksacks when Julian noticed that his codebook was missing. He started to look round the grass for it but it was nowhere to be seen. 'Perhaps it slipped out while you were crossing the stepping-stones,' George suggested. 'Do you remember that time when you wobbled a bit? Perhaps it happened then.' Julian therefore hurried back to the stones but the codebook wasn't lying there either. He was just about to return to the others when he noticed something white at the very bottom of the river. *There* was his codebook. It wouldn't be much use now, however!

If you have it, remove the CODEBOOK CARD from your RUCKSACK. Now go to 181.

272

No sooner had Dick found the stone bridge on his map than Julian announced that the three minutes were up. 'Time to be off again, I'm afraid,' he said as he slid off the wall to the ground. The short rest had helped them a little but it wasn't long before they were all feeling quite tired again. They just hoped that the caves wouldn't be much further! *Go to 168.*

273

'Let's ask that farmer over there!' Dick suggested, suddenly noticing one driving home his cows for the evening. So, as soon as they had all hurried the quarter of a mile or so to the farmer, they asked him if he knew where the airfield was. 'I should say so,' he replied rather grumpily. 'Them noisy jets sometimes scare the life out of me cows, they do. All but makes their milk turn to butter! Anyways, it's about two mile due east of 'ere.' The children immediately started looking for their compasses!

Use your COMPASS CARD to find east by placing exactly over the shape below – and with pointer touching north. Then go to

the number that appears in the window. If you don't have a
COMPASS in your RUCKSACK, you'll have to guess which of
the numbers to go to.

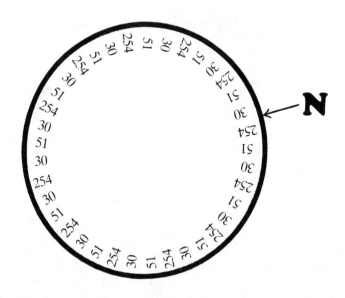

274

The Five had walked quite a bit further towards the airfield when
they arrived at a large stone archway. 'How odd – being in the
middle of nowhere!' Julian remarked. 'It must be someone's folly.
In the old days rich people often used to build strange monuments
like this just to amuse themselves!' As they passed through the
archway, Dick suggested looking it up on their maps so they would
know where they were.

Use your MAP to find which square the stone archway is in –
then follow the instruction. If you don't have a MAP in your
RUCKSACK, you'll have to guess which instruction to follow.

If you think C3	go to 83
If you think D3	go to 58
If you think D2	go to 21

'Oh, you don't need none of them gadgets!' the gypsy woman told them as they were about to use their compasses. 'Jus' follow where me arm be pointing. That's due east, towards them 'ills over there!' Thanking the gypsy woman, they set off towards the hills. As they were walking, however, Julian suddenly tripped on a small rock hidden in the grass, and fell. 'Oh no,' he cried as he heard the rattle of glass from his rucksack, 'it sounds like I've broken my binoculars!'

If you have it, remove the BINOCULARS CARD from your RUCKSACK. Now go to 104.

Eager to prove that she was the bravest, *George* volunteered to explore the airfield herself. So, she carefully squeezed through the hole in the fence and then, when the coast seemed clear, ran across the concrete towards the nearest hangar. Having checked that there was no one inside, she quickly entered the hangar, searching round. She was just about to go and try another of the buildings when she suddenly spotted a message chalked on the hangar floor. It read: *JET IS TO BE HIDDEN FIVE MILES NORTH-WEST OF*

HERE. She immediately decided to return to the others at the fence so they could look up north-west on their compasses!

*Use your **COMPASS CARD** to find this direction by placing exactly over the shape below – and with pointer touching north. Then go to the number that appears in the window. If you don't have a **COMPASS** in your **RUCKSACK**, you'll have to guess which of the numbers to go to.*

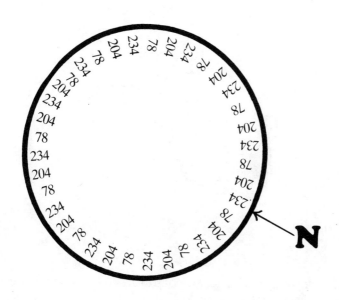

'There he goes, slinking behind that hangar in the middle!' Dick exclaimed as they watched Timmy through their binoculars. They now saw Timmy enter the hangar, anxiously waiting for him to come out again. 'Look, he's got some sort of notebook in his mouth!' George cried as Timmy finally ran back towards them. As soon as Timmy had squeezed through the hole in the fence, George took the notebook from him. 'It's someone's codebook!' she exclaimed. Turning the codebook over, they saw that there was a message scribbled on its back cover! It read: *JET TO BE HIDDEN AT THE RUINED CASTLE.*

If you don't already have it, put the CODEBOOK CARD into your RUCKSACK. Now go to 224.

Before anyone had a chance to step on to the stones, however, Anne caught their attention. 'Hey, look, there's a wooden box amongst the rocks here,' she said, bending down to investigate. 'I wonder if there's anything inside?' Opening the varnished lid, she saw that the inside was a bit like a jewellery box, with a velvety padding. In the middle of the padding was a stranged-shaped hole and she asked Julian what it was. 'It looks like a revolver case!' Julian answered rather seriously as he took it from her. Lifting the padding out, he found a slip of paper underneath with a coded message on it. He immediately went to his rucksack for his codebook!

Use your CODEBOOK CARD to find out what the message

said by decoding the instruction below. If you don't have a
CODEBOOK in your *RUCKSACK*, go to 294 instead.

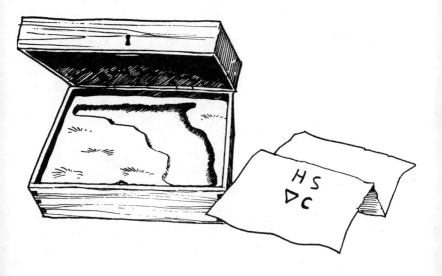

279
Just as they were putting their maps away again, Julian emerged
from the hangar. Making sure the coast was clear, he then ran all the
way back towards the fence. 'I found a message on the hangar floor!'
he panted excitedly, as he carefully squeezed through the hole
again. 'It was written on a tiny scrap of paper and said that the jet was
to be hidden at the ruined castle!' He had a bit of bad news as well,
however. He had taken his codebook along with him just in case,
carrying it in his pocket, but it was now no longer there. It must have
dropped out while he was searching the hangar!

If you have it, remove the CODEBOOK CARD from your
RUCKSACK. Now go to 42.

As soon as they had found the direction the jet was flying, they set off that way themselves. They went as quickly as their tired legs would carry them, sometimes breaking into a half-run. 'Phew, this is exhausting!' Dick panted after a mile or so. 'Let's stop for a few seconds so we can have a drink of our ginger beer. It will make our lunchboxes a little lighter as well!'

Take a PICNIC CARD from your LUNCHBOX. Now go to 35.

The ride became slightly less bumpy for a while as the jeep now joined a rough road. The commander followed it until it divided to left and right, and then drove straight across the fields again! Anne decided to look up where the road divided on her map so she would know how much further they had to go.

Use your MAP to find in which square the rough road divides – then follow the instruction. If you don't have a MAP in your RUCKSACK, you'll have to guess which instruction to follow.

If you think B1	go to 102
If you think A2	go to 52
If you think B2	go to 187

282

While they were opening their rucksacks for their binoculars, however, they heard a *woof* from just behind them. Turning round, they saw Timmy having a nice swim in the river! 'The whole idea of the stepping-stones, Timmy', George called out to him, not sure whether to be cross or laugh, 'is that they save you getting wet. There's not much point in using the stones if you're just going to jump in anyway!' Timmy looked as if he intended to stay in the river all day and so George sat on the bank, tucking into one of her sandwiches. That would soon make him come out!

Take a PICNIC CARD from your LUNCHBOX. Now go to 181.

After they had put their maps away again, they continued on their way. The ruined castle gradually became closer and closer as they walked. 'We should reach it in another half hour,' said Julian eagerly. They had only gone a few steps further, however, when he suddenly stopped, putting his hand to his head in anguish. When the others asked what was wrong, he told them that he had just realised that he wasn't carrying his lunchbox. 'I must have left it all the way back at the railway sheds!' he sighed.

Take a PICNIC CARD from your LUNCHBOX. Now go to 107. (Remember: when there are no picnic cards left in your lunchbox the game is over, and you must start again.)

284

They must have travelled a good mile towards the caves when they reached a stone bridge over a canal. They were so exhausted from all their running that they decided to have a quick rest there. 'Three minutes only!' Julian insisted as they all heaved themselves up on to the wall. 'Then we must get moving again or we might be too late!' While they were sitting on the bridge, Dick thought of looking it up on his map so they would know where they were.

Use your MAP to find which square the stone bridge is in – then follow the instruction. If you don't have a MAP in your RUCKSACK, you'll have to guess which instruction to follow.

If you think A3	go to 272
If you think B3	go to 168
If you think A2	go to 29

'I can't see him, I'm afraid,' sighed Dick, using his binoculars to look round the cave. 'The cave is much bigger than I thought, though. It seems to go on forever. So he could be there, or he could not!' Just as they were about to go and have a look into the other cave, Dick's binoculars picked out what looked like a small bicycle lamp on the ground and he ran forward to investigate. 'Hey, it works!' he exclaimed. Not only did this prove that this *was* the cave the men had come down but it also meant that they could now see where they were going! *Go to 11.*

Timmy immediately led the way down the tunnel, the others all following close behind. They must have walked a good five hundred metres or so when they suddenly heard a slight noise ahead. 'What's that?' Anne asked with alarm as they all peered into the darkness. Dick quickly looked for his binoculars to see if they would help . . .

Use your BINOCULARS CARD to try and see what caused the noise by placing exactly over the shape below – then follow the instruction. If you don't have BINOCULARS in your RUCK-SACK, go to 186 instead.

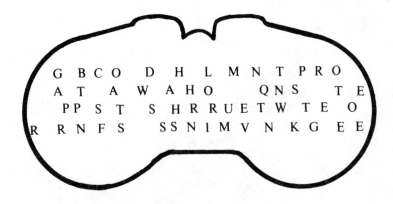

'Yes, it *is* the airfield!' Jeff said delightedly after Dick had given him his binoculars. 'I can see the runway's lights quite clearly now!' The children had a quick look through the binoculars themselves and then they all hurriedly started walking again. 'Another half mile,' Jeff told them encouragingly, 'and we'll be walking through the airfield's gate!' *Go to 67.*

Dick told Julian that it wasn't necessary to use his compass, though. The only tower in sight was on a hill half a mile to their right – so it had to be *that one* the message meant! 'Yes, how silly of me not to notice it!' Julian chuckled as he strapped his rucksack up again. He then had a good look at the round squat tower, shielding his eyes. 'I think it's one of those towers that people used to light beacons on,' he said as Anne offered them all some of her cake for a quick snack. 'The message is right about it being a good place for spying on the airfield!' What they all really wanted to know, though, was *who was it* that was doing this spying!

Take a PICNIC CARD from your LUNCHBOX. Now go to 116.

'Perhaps Jeff wrote where the caves are in another part of this diary!' Julian said suddenly, starting to turn through the pages. He had nearly reached the end of the diary when he came to a stop, flicking back a page. 'Good old Jeff – he *did*!' he exclaimed. 'Look, he's written that Billycock Caves are near the white hills.' George said that she'd never heard of *white* hills before, but suggested taking out their binoculars to see if they could spot some!

Use your BINOCULARS CARD to try and find the white hills by placing exactly over the shape below – then follow the instruction. If you don't have a BINOCULARS CARD in your RUCKSACK, go to 27 instead.

290

'Phew, that was close!' he panted as he finally reached the hole in the fence again. He had a quick drink of his ginger beer to cool himself down before telling the others about the message – or, at least, the part that wasn't in code! 'It said that the jet was to be hidden at the ruined castle,' he revealed excitedly.

Take a PICNIC CARD from your LUNCHBOX. Now go to 42.

291

'I think I might have found the airfield's observation tower!' Dick cried suddenly as they all looked through their binoculars. 'Quick, Jeff, what do you think?' Jeff carefully took hold of Dick's binoculars, lifting them up to his eyes. 'Yes, it *is* the observation tower!' he confirmed as he focused them slightly. 'I can see the radar scanner on the top. Well spotted, Dick!' They now immediately set off in that direction . . . *Go to 254.*

292

Before Julian could give the men an answer, the other one spoke. 'You've come to steal some of our butterflies, haven't you?' he snapped. 'I suppose you've heard how valuable some of them are? Now be off with you before we call the police!' The Five therefore had no option but to leave. They didn't have to walk much further, however, when they spotted a farmer riding around on his tractor. 'Let's ask *him* the way,' George suggested. 'Perhaps he'll be rather more friendly!' So they all ran towards the farmer.

Throw THE FAMOUS FIVE DICE to decide who is to reach him first.

JULIAN thrown	go to 113
DICK thrown	go to 203
GEORGE thrown	go to 233
ANNE thrown	go to 69
TIMMY thrown	go to 158
MYSTERY thrown	go to 246

293

When they were ready with their codebooks, however, they saw that the scrap of paper was gone. The wind must have blown it off the barbed wire! The children returned disappointedly to the question of who was going to crawl through the fence, with *Julian* eventually volunteering. When he saw the coast was clear, he dashed across the open concrete towards the nearest hangar. The hangar appeared empty and so he crept inside to explore it. He was just about to leave the hangar to explore another of the buildings when he discovered a tiny message chalked on to the back wall. It read: *JET TO BE HIDDEN AT THE RUINED CASTLE*. Rushing back to the fence, he excitedly told the others about this discovery. He then had a long drink of his ginger beer to cool himself down!

Take a PICNIC CARD from your LUNCHBOX. Now go to 224.

294

While Julian was looking for his codebook, however, the slip of paper fluttered out of the box in a gust of wind. 'Quick, catch it before it goes into the river!' Anne cried with alarm as it was blown along the water's edge. 'Oh no, we're too late!' she sighed, only a couple of seconds later. To make up for their disappointment at losing the message, they decided to have a piece of cake each from their lunchboxes before continuing.

Take a PICNIC CARD from your LUNCHBOX. Now go to 181.

295

Fortunately, the plane circled round a couple of times and so Jeff had time to work out the code on its wings. 'It said that the foreign pilot is to parachute down at ten o'clock,' he informed the children breathlessly as the plane now disappeared. 'You know which foreign pilot that must be, don't you? The one who is to fly my jet abroad! That plane is obviously going to drop him – and that message must have been for the people who are to pick him up!' **Go to 155.**

296

When the children tried to decode the message on the rocks, though, they found that it didn't make any sense! 'The two men must have spotted Jeff writing it,' Julian guessed, 'and altered all the symbols to spite him. That's why the message comes out as a complete load of nonsense!' To make up for their disappointment, Dick took out a slice of his cake, breaking off a piece for each of them. 'Those men sound really mean, don't they?' he said as he handed the pieces out.

Take a PICNIC CARD from your LUNCHBOX. Now go to 228. (Remember: when there are no picnic cards left in your lunchbox the game is over, and you must start again.)

297

As soon as they had found south-east on their compasses, they started to walk the twelve paces in that direction. They had just reached the final pace when Julian kicked something on the ground. 'The lamp, if I'm not mistaken!' he remarked as he bent down to investigate. It certainly *felt* like a lamp and his fingers tried to find the switch. 'Ah, that's better!' he exclaimed as a bright beam suddenly came on. 'Now we can see where we're going!' **Go to 184.**

While they were looking for their codebooks, though, Dick suddenly noticed how short the candle was. 'It might not last much longer,' he told the others anxiously. 'Perhaps we ought to forget about the message for the time being and save the candle for looking for Jeff!' The others agreed with him and so they explored deeper and deeper into the cave. George munched one of her sandwiches on the way to take her mind off how scary the place was!

Take a PICNIC CARD from your LUNCHBOX. Now go to 11.

'Be careful, it gets quite deep here!' Anne said over her shoulder to the others as she led them across the stepping-stones. Fortunately, though, the stones were quite wide and firm and so they all reached the other bank without slipping in. Before they continued on their way, George suggested looking up the river on their maps. It would show them roughly where they were!

Use your MAP to find which square the river is in – then follow the instruction. If you don't have a MAP in your RUCKSACK, you'll have to guess which instruction to follow.

If you think C1	go to 271
If you think D1	go to 44
If you think E1	go to 181

'I can't see that stone cross anywhere!' Anne tutted as they all closely examined their maps. Julian insisted they keep looking for it, though, saying that something as large as that must be shown somewhere. 'It's probably staring us in the face!' he added, starting to examine his map all over again. ***Go to 16.***

'It works out as: *THIS IS THE CAVE TO EXPLORE*,' Dick announced thoughtfully when he was the first to finish decoding the message on the map. 'I wonder what it means exactly – and who wrote it?' They all scratched their heads for a moment and then Julian suddenly realised. 'I bet it was written by Jeff when the men weren't looking!' he exclaimed. 'This map was probably the only thing he had to scribble it on. Anyway, it's obviously so his rescuers realise that it's *this* cave he has been taken into, and not that other one.'

If you don't already have it, put the MAP into your RUCK-SACK. Now go to 11.

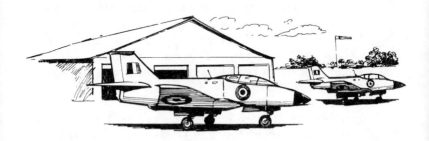